GERMANY – THE NEW PHOTOGRAPHY 1927–33

Albert Renger-Patzsch *Blastfurnace air-heaters, Herrenwyk*

GERMANY
THE NEW PHOTOGRAPHY
1927-33

Documents and essays
selected and edited by David Mellor

Arts Council of Great Britain

GERMANY – THE NEW PHOTOGRAPHY 1927–33
First published 1978 by the Arts Council of Great Britain
Produced by Barry Lane
This selection copyright © David Mellor
Copyright acknowledgements of items in this volume are found on page 133
Designed by Roger Huggett/Sinc.
Printed in Great Britain by Lund Humphries.
ISBN 0 7287 0185 5

A list of Arts Council publications, including all exhibition catalogues in print,
can be obtained from the Publications Office, Arts Council of Great Britain,
105 Piccadilly, London W1V 0AU

Contents

7   David Mellor
Preface

PART I   ORIGINAL DOCUMENTS, STATEMENTS AND CRITICISMS
THE NEW OBJECTIVITY –
RENGER-PATZSCH AND BLOSSFELDT

9   Carl Georg Heise 1928
Preface to A. Renger-Patzsch, *Die Welt ist schön*

15   Albert Renger-Patzsch 1929
Photography and Art

17   Karl Nierendorf 1928
Preface to Karl Blossfeldt, *Urformen der Kunst*

20   Walter Benjamin 1928
New things about plants
A review of Karl Blossfeldt, *Urformen der Kunst*

23   Paul Nash 1932
Photography and Modern Art
A review of Karl Blossfeldt, *Art Forms in Nature*

'HERE COMES THE NEW PHOTOGRAPHER!'

25   Werner Gräff 1929
Foreword to *Es kommt der neue Fotograf!*

FRANZ ROH AND THE 'FILM AND FOTO' EXHIBITION

29   Franz Roh 1929
Mechanism and expression: the essence and value of photography
Introduction to *foto-auge*

35   A. Kraszna-Krausz 1929
Exhibition in Stuttgart, June 1929, and its Effects
- Extract from a review of the *Film und Foto* exhibition

37   Oswell Blakeston 1930
A review of Franz Roh and Jan Tschichold, *foto-auge*

39   Franz Roh 1930
The literary dispute about photography
Theses and antitheses to theme 'Mechanism and expression'
Introduction to *Aenne Biermann:* Fototek 2

43   Oswell Blakeston 1931
Recapitulation
A review of Franz Roh's *Fototek* series

POLITICAL PERSPECTIVES AND THE 'WORKER PHOTOGRAPHER'

45   Max Dortu c.1930
Come Before the Camera

47   Edwin Hoernle 1930
The Working Man's Eye

51   Willi Münzenberg 1931
Tasks and Objectives

FACES AND SOCIAL TYPES – SANDER AND LERSKI

55   Alfred Döblin 1929
Introduction to August Sander, *Antlitz der Zeit*

61   Curt Glaser 1931
Introduction to Helmar Lerski, *Köpfe des Alltags*

65   Kenneth Macpherson 1931
As Is
A review of Helmar Lerski, *Köpfe des Alltags*

THE CRITICISM OF WALTER BENJAMIN

69   Walter Benjamin 1931
Extract from *A Short History of Photography*

PART II   CURRENT PERSPECTIVES

77   Beaumont Newhall 1977
Photo Eye of the 1920s: The Deutsche Werkbund Exhibition of 1929

87   Herbert Molderings 1978
Urbanism and Technological Utopianism
Thoughts on the Photography of Neue Sachlichkeit and The Bauhaus

95   Brian Stokoe 1978
Renger-Patzsch: New Realist Photographer

101   Ute Eskildsen 1978
Photography and the Neue Sachlichkeit Movement

113   David Mellor 1978
London – Berlin – London: a cultural history
The Reception and Influence of the New German
Photography in Britain 1927—33

133   Acknowledgements

134   Index

Preface

This book is intended as a source book of material gathered from the fundamental documents of German photography around 1930. Most of the original documents first appeared in books and magazines that have not subsequently been republished, and many are translated here for the first time. By collecting these texts together in one volume, there is now the opportunity of examining the multiplicity of tendencies – across Bauhaus experimentation, the New Objectivity and the Worker Photographers – that comprised the extraordinary developments in vanguard photography during the short period in Germany at the end of the 1920s and the beginning of the 1930s. This complex cluster of photographic theories and styles has been placed, for the purposes of this book, under the generic heading of 'The New Photography' – a term which had a wide currency in Germany at that moment. Yet the German 'New Photography' has remained one of the last areas of modernist art and culture to be mapped and it is hoped that these documents will form the basis for continued analysis and further historical research into such major and unjustifiably, neglected figures as Helmar Lerski or Werner Gräff.

There are two important omissions that, it should be noted, have been published elsewhere. The expansion of photo-journalism, while referred to on many occasions in the assembled texts is not here directly represented by primary documents. Secondly, Walter Benjamin's interpretation of the political identity of New Objectivity, and of Albert Renger-Patzsch's photography in particular, found in his essay *The Author as Producer* (1934) appeared in *Understanding Brecht* (New Left Books, London 1973).

The texts begin with the two masters of New Objectivity photography, Albert Renger-Patzsch and Karl Blossfeldt. The important introductions to their photo-books, as well as contemporary reviews from Germany and Britain are included. Then the experimental departures of Werner Gräff and the writings of critic and historian Franz Roh are located in the period of the influential *Film und Foto* exhibition at Stuttgart in 1929; (the original, highly idiosyncratic translation of Roh's *foto-auge* introduction has been retained).

This is followed by a selection of documents from the Worker Photographer movement. Two distinguished photographers, August Sander and Helmar Lerski – both concerned with new forms of portraiture – are next represented and the first part of the book is closed by Walter Benjamin's perceptions of contemporary photography in 1931.

The second part of this collection comments on the period from the point of view of today through the medium of historical essays. Beaumont Newhall contributes an essay which underlines the importance of the 1929 *Film und Foto* exhibition. Herbert Molderings and Ute Eskildsen offer surveys of the theoretical issues and photographic practice across the range of late twenties and early thirties German photography; while Brian Stokoe examines Albert Renger-Patzsch in a critical case study of the New Objectivity. In the concluding essay, I have tried to trace the diffusion of the new German modes into British photography and culture.

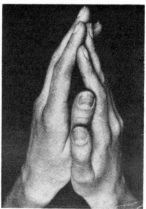
Advertisement for A. Renger-Patzsch *Die Welt ist schön*

8

Carl Georg Heise 1928

Preface to Albert Renger-Patzsch, *Die Welt ist schön*

Whether we admit it or not, the fact that the world is beautiful is a precondition for art of all kinds. Much is spoken about ugliness in art, about new art forms which are more concerned with objectivity than with beauty. Basically, however, the cults of ugliness and functionality only appear to be a denial of beauty; in fact they are no more than a revolution in aesthetic perception, an attempt at the creation of a new concept of beauty. In the words of Deri: "Beauty is that indefinable something which has the power of enriching a relatively small group of people on a strong emotional level at the moment of perception." Photographs, however, assuming that they are as vital, bold and creative as those of Albert Renger-Patzsch, have the ability of enriching a far larger circle of people, who may be entirely different from each other, and uniting them in an enthusiasm similar to that aroused by the painting of our time. Leaving aside the question of whether the new horizons of photographic creation can justifiably be regarded as art in the highest and most exact meaning of the word, the fact remains that the world of these photographs is beautiful. The following is an attempt at an explanation of the reason for this beauty.

Plants
Who, apart from Renger-Patzsch, is in the habit of observing a flower so closely? The botanist. A close relationship to botany is a great advantage, for – like the botanist – the photographer isolates the characteristic fragment from the multiplicity of the whole, underlines the essential elements and eliminates that which could lead to a deconcentration into the complexity of the whole. He captures the observer's attention and directs it to the strange beauty of organic growth. He expresses in a visual form that which the scientist can only describe. He reveals the fascination of matter: the dull shine of the skin of a grape, for example, or the minute delicate hairs of the calyx of the Echynopsis cupreata, the beauty of the colours: the viewer can perceive the somewhat gaudy radiance of the dahlia so dominant in autumn, and the expressive impact of isolated forms: the Euphorbia grandicornis cuts through the dark image like a streak of lightning, and uncanny shoots run rampant on the ripe rye straw. The strangeness of the foreign plants is as convincingly evident as the familiarity of the local vegetation. Particularly interesting is the fact that plants or fragments of plants appear only very rarely in an overdimensioned form, and the photographer never seeks a new artistic form for its own sake if it does not serve to elucidate the object itself. The plant is characterized and never misused as a complacent plaything. Characterization in its most pregnant form is also evident in the photograph of the papaya, seen from below, in order to emphasize the unique growth of the branches and leaves – a 'system of canals'. The image section is selected and limited in such a way that the positioning of the twigs and branches, together with the shimmering bars of the glass roof, results in a bold lattice-work of unique graphic beauty. This is the culmination: the plant is depicted in its typical beauty and, at the same time, extended into a lineal ornamentation of fascinating tension, without losing anything of its own natural essence. The camera is capable of perceiving certain natural objects more clearly than the eye: the picture of the salicornia, the first sign of plant

life on newly gained land, is full of an awareness of the formal unity between plant growth and shadow. This too, is a legitimate fascination, for it is the shadow which so effectively emphasizes the trembling uncertainty of the fearful, hasty plant growth.

Animals and People

It is characteristic of Renger-Patzsch that he is not a portrait photographer, or at least that he never made a career out of this most popular specialized field. After all, is it not true to say that animals are more interesting than human beings? His photographs would seem to give this impression. Here, too, like in his flower pictures, he underlines the typical aspect of his subject. The portrait of the baboon has a regal dignity; the animal's eyes are fixed firmly on the distance, and it wears its fur like a royal insignia. But nothing is intentionally posed, no 'picturesque' retouching obscures the strict objectivity of the image, and the character of matter is uncompromisingly sharp. The head of the adder is so integrated in the coils of the snake's body that the picture appears to be filled with ornaments composed of scales and the viewer's imagination is expanded – uncannily – into infinity. Thus the photograph makes a statement about the species over and above the single snake. The herd, the collection of animals, is almost more suggestive. In the picture of the sheep pressed closely together with but one head visible in front of countless backs, the photographer succeeds in creating a surprise effect: he freezes movement. The viewer seems to see these animals in endless rows, jostling one against the other, their backs visible as one large wave, spreading out over the field like an avalanche. It is this, and not any similarity to the effect of painting, which makes this image a work of art. And to Renger-Patzsch, human beings are like animals. He searches for that which is typical of the species. A little Somali girl, her head as bare as a billiard ball, shows the face of a child formed more by the forces of nature than by the human mind. And the Maori mummy awakens the ghosts of an extinct race.

Landscapes

Landscape photographs are dangerous, they are too seductive to effects which are imitations of paintings. Every amateur has tried his hand at pictures in the Dachau or Worpswede mood, or sea or mountainscapes in the style of certain fashionable painters. The dubious element lies in the imitation of the artistic style by means of the 'Edeldruckverfahren' (art printing process), not in the expression of the subject through typical selection, lighting, cropping and impact of reproduction. This task of the artistically trained eye alone, which must be completed before the start of the technical process, gives – for example – 'the winter forest' the determining element of its compelling beauty; technical skill is by no means impeded by interference of personal taste, it merely uses to the full the possibilities of an exact exploitation of the tonal values, so that – in spite of an almost ornamental use of the image surface – a spatial suggestion of almost overwhelming impact is achieved. How radiant the white is, how mysteriously the grey tones of the snow relate to one another! A close-up of a single tree can, however, conjure up the same intensive atmosphere of sylvan nature as the picture of densely packed trunks. The fact that a fragment can symbolize the whole, and that enjoyment and empathy are mutually exalting when the imagination is forced to collaborate in the experience – this is an area in which landscape photography offers a multitude of possibilities. Willows in the foreground, more willows in the mid-distance, farmland surrounding the trees – this is the northern German plain landscape; the wave, captured at the moment of its maximum movement, this is the sea; a snow-covered fir tree, broken by the storm, this is the world of winter. These are pictures of the life of the earth in the sense of Caspar David Friedrich. In this way, a relationship between the painter and the photographer is both possible and fruitful – not because of the style of the image, but because of the similarity of conception. The skill of the execution should not be overlooked: with what sure and certain perception – for example in the picture of the path through the vineyard – has the photographer enlivened the foreground (with shadows, with sharply focused vegetation!), and with what perfection has he placed the static beside the mobile in the stage setting – unsharpness merging into sharpness, each increasing the impact of the other. And the fact that it is not merely an exaggerated stylization by the artist but also a sharpness of photographic seeing which conjures up the fantastic in everyday nature, this is proved again and again by Renger-Patzsch's camera.

Material

This is unquestionably the photographer's domain. Van Dyck painted silk in such a way that the viewer was almost able to hear it rustling. Since the 19th century, however, the ambition of our leading masters is no longer directed towards brilliant representations of material. Since the invention of photography, painters tend to avoid all areas in which mechanical methods could represent serious competition. The whole development of modern art is – to a far greater degree than is usually admitted – influenced by the flood of images from all areas accessible to the camera. To describe a painting as being 'photographically faithful' is to condemn it utterly. This would explain the sudden failure of portrait painters, as well as the disintegration of matter up to the point where the object ceases to exist. But is it true to say that photography sought these unoccupied areas? At any rate, it certainly took its time. It was seduced into imitating painting, into artistic simulation and obscuration, although the camera was in fact committed to the utmost accuracy. Thus a grotesque situation arose in which photography began chasing after painting – which, for its part fled in fear before photography, and certain aspects of high aesthetic value remained allegedly inartistic and entirely devoid of neoteric fulfilment. It is much to the credit of Renger-Patzsch – and many who came after him – that he aspired to create maximally clear and sharp photographic images of material. The eye of the viewer is enthralled by long-missed pleasures: the photograph of a simple material from the Hameln workshops; of glass, delicate and brittle; of beechwood, coarsely chopped and rough; and of coffee-beans, hard and black and shiny. The charm of these images is inexhaustible. Stacked tiles fill the page with runic signs, suspended between order and confusion as in a water-colour by Klee. Shoe-trees stand at attention like a military regiment. Photographs of this kind are both beautiful and useful, and highly effective as advertising images for prospectuses and posters. Justifiably, they oust any drawn or painted representation. In the case of faithful material portrayals, technically exact reproductions are always preferable to artistic depictions. And although this complies with a sober, business-like attitude, the necessary changeover from bad habits is a slow process: one of the best images in this area was rejected by the client. But the march of development cannot be checked.

Architecture

Architectural photographs are attempts at the portrayal and interpretation of buildings. For this reason, the artistic character of the subject must be far more binding for the photographer than in the case of photographs of nature, flowers, animals or landscapes. Here, too, many 'sins' have been committed. Pictures of skyscrapers from eccentric angles lose their convincing descriptive-ness, although they may gain a certain originality. 'Clever' cropping is only justified when it directs the viewer's attention to an essential element. When, for example, bannisters follow and accentuate the curve of a staircase, the photographer is justified in emphasizing them. And when he seeks and accen-tuates the spot in a medieval cathedral – aided by glaring light – where the Romanesque beginnings join suddenly and harshly with the later, late-Gothic period, he does so in order to draw attention to a fragment of history as well as to the characteristic beauty of the building. In all objectivity, this is a creative achievement. A view of the backs of sad suburban houses, a still-life of roofs and chimneys, is more than a simple portrayal of buildings, more than a characteristic image of poverty and city architectural un-culture: the transla-tion of what the photographer saw in everyday reality into a black-and-white image spurs the viewer on to seek a visual excitement which he previously passed by unaware, a play of tension between sooty chimneys and blinking lights, delicate, densely packed horizontals and massive verticals, light and dark walls and windows. It is no coincidence that these images recall a famous painting by one of the painters of the 'New Objectivity' school. The aesthetic attitude is the same in both cases.

Technique

The concept of 'beauty of technique' is no longer new. Technical works which are 'in fact' ugly gain a certain aesthetic charm when viewed in the light of their usefulness. This beauty is not quite on a level with the more usual concept of beauty; it is, as it were, a second class beauty. It is only lately that the much more basic concept that this new beauty is in the process of reforming our entire aesthetic attitude is gaining ground. Not that everything that is beautiful must be useful – on the contrary: we notice with surprise that even the techni-cian only appears to be concerned solely with the usefulness of his inventions, and that in fact he is unconsciously inspired by a new feeling for beauty when searching for new forms. The technical attitude rules the world, and there still exists well-guarded paradisical gardens in which old-fashioned but very genuine flowers of beauty grow, separate from all technical thought; neverthe-less, the majority of creative persons are too strongly permeated by the spirit of technology to allow their work to escape its influence entirely. The rhythm of technology fills all work. The works of technology should not adapt to an existing aesthetic code; through them, our concept of beauty gains a basically altered character. Renger-Patzsch's industrial photographs clearly show that it is possible to regard a machine or an industrial plant as no less beautiful than nature or a work of art. There is no longer a difference of niveau, only a difference in quality. When the grabhook of a crane emphasizes its function, then it is beautiful. But Renger-Patzsch's pictures portray more than the for-mal beauty of an object. The chain of insulators hangs radiant and lively before an endless sky, symbolic of its function. Three cranes are shown in such a way that the divergence of lines conjures up the sequence of their motion. The wire of the cableway speaks of the tempo of its fabrication. It is virgin soil, this new beauty, and it is the task of the master to exploit it fully.

A Coloured World

No, things are are not inherently ugly or beautiful; the creative eye can 'wrench' hidden beauty from them, as Dürer once put it. There is nothing which is entirely devoid of beauty. Take the fishing nets hanging out to dry on the railings of a bridge for example. Renger-Patzsch's art turns them into a huge decoration. Although it would be wrong to regard this as no more than a playful delight in arrangement, it is true to say that a heightened form is always extracted from the essence of the objects. The up-and-down of the steps of the bridge with the densely hanging nets gives an insight into the rhythm of the daily work served by the nets. The Russian swing, still under construction, conjures up a concentrated impression of the jubilation and poverty of the annual fair with its juxtaposition of splendid, towering wheels and scaffolding and cheap furnishings. A hand corn-mill, still used today in the North Frisian Islands, presents a picture of primitive usefulness and obsolete tradition with its expressively contrasted surfaces. But it would be wrong to attempt to mould these bold voyages into a truly colourful world into mere formulas. If it were possible to reproduce their content in a literary form, they would not be so visually impressive. A frozen waterfall, reeds with trembling reflections, groynes encrusted with mussels and small forms of sea vegetation – Renger-Patzsch's camera makes these the basis for pictures invested with a strange and many-sided life of their own, objective and formally fascinating. The picture of the reeds is reminiscent of a Japanese pen-and-ink drawing; it owes much of its impact and decorative effectiveness, of this there can be no doubt, to the reduction of the original colour image to black and white. It would be a mistake to insist on colour photography (except in cases of absolutely faithful reproduction of the subject), for it would reduce the legitimate artistic effect to a minimum. This world is colourful in the highest, translated sense – but the sense is easier to discover and more effectively emphasized when it is expressed in the new sphere of black and white surfaces, half dematerialized through the absence of colour, removed, as it were, to a spiritual plane. In this context, it is worthwhile drawing attention to the danger attached to this new concept by the possibility of a too severe 'cropping' of perception. Much that is hidden comes to life, but much that has been effective since time immemorial falls apart. It has become usual to photograph details of works of art. There is hardly a book about medieval sculpture which does not contain photographs of single heads. This may well heighten the aesthetic effect, but it robs the sculpture of its sacred power – for example when the head and body of the crucified Christ are depicted on the lap of his grieving mother without the inclusion of her suffering face. The only possible excuse lies in the fact that the old symbols have lost their meaning and that all that remains is a purely artistic way of seeing. The camera opens up new fields of pious wonderment and destroys others.

The Symbol

Our highest inherited concepts are beginning to become obscure. We must endow them with new life. Edgar Dacqué has written an excellent book on the subject of symbols. "In order to be a true and living concept", states Dacqué, "the symbol must bear within it an essential being which reflects upon the mind, reflects with increasing power according to the degree to which the mind opens to its inner sense. For this reason, true symbols are like living and life-giving beings which carry their inner world with them constantly and finally, and not always at once, lead back to the source of all existence." These words can justifiably be applied to Renger-Patzsch's finest photographs, the last ones in this book. They are true symbols. Nevertheless, we should not forget that it is basically nature and created life itself which bears within it symbolic power of this kind, and that the work of the photographer does not create symbols but merely makes them visible! But the pointing of the way towards independent seeing and to the strengthening of our feeling for the reflection of the universe in single objects of creation – this alone is a valuable service which can hardly be over-estimated. Since the powerful symbols of our forefathers are beginning to lose their meaning, it is of the greatest importance that we should re-learn to recognize the inexhaustible life itself in all its parts as symbols. Naturally, the examples selected are arbitrary, like examples always must be. Other pictures could easily have been chosen in place of these. All that remains is a brief attempt to give an idea of the various possibilities by means of which the observed object can be heightened to a symbolic image. It is often only the cropped section which reveals the characteristic fragment of the whole that brings about this heightening, as for example in the case of the chimneys of the blast furnace plant, the mountain pines or the nets in the fishing boat – here underlined by the brilliant inclusion of the large sweep of the net as a guiding line for the eye of the observer which conjures up the effect of rocking motion. The cropped section of the Gothic arch, too, is more than a mere means of producing an artistic effect – although this is certainly present: it is a suggestive elucidation of the laws inherent in Gothic arches in general. The upright rows of irons, this 'phalanx' of identical tools, becomes a symbol of mass production. But there are even more meaningful symbols. The Zwinger steps in Dresden, with their sweeping curves, recall the waves of the sea and thus uncannily suggest the primeval basis of all architectural imagination which draws its creative strength from the forms of organic nature. The centre stalk of an agave provides a complete contrast: a fragment of natural growth, boldly curved and yet firmly in place like a modern building. The last picture is of a woman's hands, raised, laid lightly over one another. Who can fail to recognize the symbolic character of this picture which speaks with an insistence far more powerful than words! We perceive the human organism as destined to varied activities by virtue of the complicated mobility of its limbs, but bound to interweave in the interests of a higher cause – like the simple uniting of the ten fingers of two hands to a larger, integrated form, the proof of a highly unschematic and yet entirely unequivocal aspiration to a higher goal. Proof? Here words fail. It is impossible to describe that which the abundance of mysterious hints at the meaning of the universe brings to life. He who has eyes to see, let him see.

Albert Renger-Patzsch *Ruhr district* 1930

Albert Renger-Patzsch 1929

Photography and Art

Statement in *Das Deutsche Lichtbild*

There was a time when one looked over one's shoulder with an ironical smile at the photographer and when photography as a profession seemed almost invariably a target for ridicule. That time is now over. A whole number of people of cultivated taste, technical ability and well-developed formal talent have made photography into a matter of serious artistic concern.

The question of whether photography *can be regarded as art or not* has given rise to much verbal and written discussion. However, it seems pointless to me to attempt to determine the question either way. After all, one can prove everything: that it is art and that it is not, that it assumes an intermediate position, that one must extend the concept of art to take account of photography, and so on. Basically that is a question which, for reasons of organisation, might interest the editor of an encyclopaedia of conversation, but it has nothing to do with the real issues. Therefore we shall refrain from any attempt at classification.

But photography *exists* and has done for nearly a hundred years now. It has acquired an immense significance for modern man, many thousands of people live from it and through it, it exerts an immense influence on wide sections of the population by means of film, it has given rise to the illustrated press, it provides true-to-life illustrations in most works of a scientific nature, in short, modern life is no longer thinkable without photography.

There is not the slightest doubt that graphic art has been obliged to surrender to the camera much territory in which it was previously absolutely sovereign, and not only for reasons of economy, but because in many instances photography works faster, and with greater precision and greater objectivity than the hand of the artist. Whilst art used often to be concerned with representation – it was, after all, impossible to report by means of photographs – modern artists have drawn the right conclusions from the changes which have taken place, and have logically attempted to fashion art in absolute terms. Modern art can no longer pursue representational goals. Photography has clearly set off at a fine pace in the progress it has made, and there is not the slightest doubt that the *photographic industry* has tackled all the difficulties with untiring energy, and that, hand in hand with science, it has performed a labour in the last thirty years which must fill us with admiration.

It cannot be denied that the practising professional photographer and the photography enthusiast were not quite equal to the American pace at which this development took place. Photography was presented with opportunities, firstly because of the way in which photographic technique was perfected, and secondly because of the way in which graphic art, which seeks to solve absolute problems of form, colour and space, voluntarily retired from the field – and these opportunities have by no means been fully exploited in the way that one might have expected.

Quite the reverse. Time and again people have been only too keen *to compete with art.* They perfect what they regard as high quality printing processes, they improve negatives and positives, or rather they *make them worse by improving them*, in order *to turn a good photograph into a bad picture*, unaware of the fact that the very photographic materials and photographic techniques themselves permit one to achieve far greater variety.

Instead of studying these techniques in all their refinements, in order then to attain the greatest achievements in the field of photography, they mix the techniques in an irresponsible way, and one can often not tell from a production of this kind which part is due to photographic technique, and which to the drawing skills of its creator.

One of the oldest laws of art and craftsmanship is that one should maintain the unity of technique and materials. By using the paintbrush and the pencil in photography they interfere with this unity, and instead of coming closer to the work of art as intended, they come into conflict with one of the first laws of art. With great skill they will perhaps achieve a certain superficial resemblance to an artistic technique, but anyone who is familiar with such things will soon notice what they have attempted to do.

Without wishing to assign a particular status to photography, which, as pointed out above, seems to us unimportant, I should nevertheless like to assert that photography provides the most varied abilities with *opportunities to express themselves in the most varied ways*, which may have nothing to do with the technique of the graphic artist but which nevertheless depend to the greatest possible extent on the taste, technical ability and creative talent of the photographer.

Just as the graphic artist depends on the materials in which he is working, and, for example, an artist using etching materials to achieve the effects of lithography would become the object of scorn, so the photographer has to know his materials and their limitations, if, rather than achieve successes with the uninitiated, his aim is to reach the greatest heights in his field.

If we disregard colour photography, which is not yet sufficiently technically advanced, then these limitations are as follows: *all shades of light from the brightest to the deepest shadow, line, plane and space.*

In order to fashion these into vital form and shape he has the media of light (natural or artificial), lens, plate, developer, copying paper, his eyes and his photographic taste. These tools open up to him – within the limitations placed on photographic technique – a thousand creative forms. If he is a great master of the technique, then in a moment he can conjure up things which will call for days of effort from the artist, or may even be totally inaccessible to him, in realms which are the natural home of photography. Whether it be as the sovereign mistress of the fleeting moment, or in the analysis of individual phases of rapid movement, whether it be to create a permanent record of the transient beauty of flowers, or to reproduce the dynamism of modern technology.

Karl Nierendorf 1928

Preface to Karl Blossfeldt, *Urformen der Kunst*

Art and Nature are two phenomena so intimately bound up as to be inseparable, yet they cannot be contained within the confines of a single concept. Natural forms are governed by some fixed and eternal force, and shaped, as a result, by constant repetition of a flow of events. These events may be modified by climatic change or transformations of soil conditions, but the basic pattern will remain. Ferns and horsetails have not changed for thousands of years; only their size has altered with the change of the earth's atmosphere. What distinguishes the work of art from the work of nature is the creative act: the peculiar stamp of an individually fashioned form, the newly created rather than the predetermined or repeated form. Art springs directly from the prevailing forces of the time in which it is made and is its visual expression.

Just as the timelessness of a blade of grass, as a symbol of the eternal laws of life, appears monumental and worthy of respect, so the work of art impresses by the singularity of its concentrated expression – it is an arc linking the two poles of past and future. From the Assyrian temple to the stadium of today, from the meditating Buddha to Rodin's *Thinker*, from Japanese coloured woodcuts to contemporary copper etching plates – all of these things created by man, bear witness to the spirit of their age. Each generation's relation to Nature, to God and to mathematics is documented in its artistic creation; and more powerfully the present is contained in a work, the more assured is its eternal value.

If man, over thousands of years were to produce the same architecture and the same art forms, without change, his creations would be the same as those constructions built by bees and termites, the complicated nests of certain birds, the spider's web or the snail's shell. However, what elevates man above other creatures is his ability to change through his own mental efforts – those efforts which rendered the world of the medieval Catholic different from that of the classical Greek. Just as Nature, in the eternal monotony of regeneration and decline, is the embodiment of a dark and overwhelming secret, so art is a similarly inconceivable secondary creation, organically born of human hearts and minds, from which springs a yearning for permanence, for eternity. It embodies a desire to capture the spiritual countenance of the age in stone, bronze, wood and in images so that the spirit, threatened with extinction in the confusion of time, will last beyond life and death.

At the present time (1928) we are seeing how contemporary youth, in its rebellion against relentless dedication to material things and intellectualization, is devoting its attentions to the elemental forces of Nature. Sport has become a powerful, world-wide phenomenon providing a seemingly necessary balance. A new kind of man is appearing: a creature who enjoys play, is confident in both air and water, tanned by the sun and determined to discover and open up a brighter world for himself. The pleasing and healing power of light, fresh air and sun are being recognized. People are striving for enlightenment and inspiration in both body and mind, and in this transformation of their lives are embracing an active and direct relationship with Nature. At the same time a new kind of architecture is breaking free from the cavernous stone piles of our fathers, opening up new ranges of vision by means of light, glass walls, linking the house organically with the garden, the fantastic richness of which has only been made possible by the

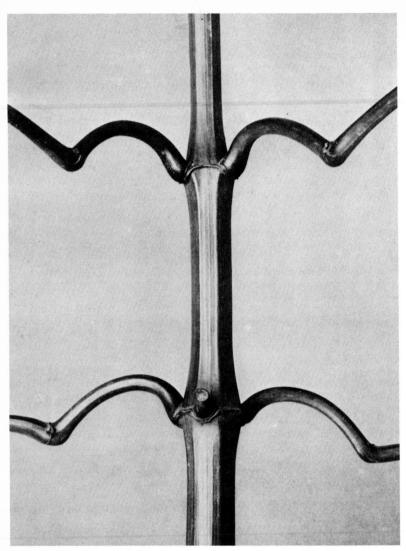

Karl Blossfeldt *Impatiens glanduligera, Hardy Indian Balsam stem with ramifications*

careful planting and the cultivation of new strains of flowers. Beyond the garden the car establishes close contact between town and country; after a protracted alienation from Nature man is now nearer to it than ever. In film, thanks to the time-lapse cine camera, he can watch the swelling and shrinking, the breathing and the growth of plants. The microscope reveals whole systems of life in drops of water, and the instruments of the observatory open up the infinity of the universe. It is technology which affords us the new means for artistic development. 'The struggles of the spirit are fought out on canvas.' These words were highly appropriate for the nineteenth century, of which the highest artistic achievements lay in painting. Now, the instruments of struggle are iron, concrete, steel, light and ether waves. Our architecture, works of engineering, cars and aeroplanes, like our films, radio and photography, all are potentially of a high aesthetic standard. And there are a thousand indications that the oft-bemoaned triumph of technology does not constitute the triumph of matter; rather, that it is the creative spirit now manifesting itself under a new guise.

It is not surprising then, that when a work appears which has been realized with the help of photographic apparatus, that a link may be detected between Art and Nature, a link of more striking immediacy than has ever been seen before. In his hundreds of plant pictures, solely through multiple magnification of plant specimens and without retouching or artifical effects, Professor Blossfeldt has shown the close relationship between forms created by man and those created by Nature. For the artist looking at Nature through the eye of the camera, a world reveals itself which embraces all the styles and moods which can be seen in the art of the past – from dramatic intensity to powerful calm – even to the expression of lyrical inner inspiration. Here can be observed the delicacy of a Rococo ornament, the severity of a Renaissance chandelier, the mystically tangled scrollwork of flamboyant Gothic, domes, towers, and the noble shafts of columns – a whole exotic language of architecture. Crosiers embossed in gold, wrought iron trellises, rich sceptres: all these man-made forms find their original form in the world of plants. Even dance finds a parallel in the unfurling bud, of which the heart-stirring, child-like gestures give a pure, spiritual thrill, conjuring up a dream picture, a vision, which slowly descends to our earthly world of flowers. The picture of this germinating impulse bears extraordinarily clear witness to the oneness of the artificially created form with life itself. Dance, which is linked to the flow of natural events in time, only becomes Art through the repetition of the regular and precisely determined rhythms of movement in Nature. Its gestures cannot be given permanence so they must be extracted from the constantly repeated flow of Nature's development. The plant buds, feeling no such temporal pressure, endlessly adopt eternal forms in order to simply unfurl. These forms can be likened to the positions of an inspired human body. Dance has consciously to distill this spiritual expression, approaching it through the element of time – a condition inherent in Art.

Far more enchanting, though, than this aesthetic experience is the final realization of the hidden powers of Creation – in the ebb and flow of which we, as creatures of Nature, are inextricably caught. The work produced by successive generations as witness to their existence, and the most transient and delicate of natural forms, each must conform to the natural laws which fashion everything.

If, for the first time, Blossfeldt's work has demonstrated the increasingly evident connections between the great and the small in the created world, then, in its own way, it is contributing to the most important task which confronts us today: that is to record the profound sense of *this* present which in all preserves – in life, art and technology – consists of a striving for a new oneness.

Walter Benjamin 1928

New things about plants

A review of Karl Blossfeldt, *Urformen der Kunst*

Criticism is a very convivial activity – any good reader will spurn the judgement of critics. But what he will very much enjoy is the delightfully bad habit of participating, uninvited, in whatever book is being reviewed at the time. Criticism consists of introducing a book so that it beckons like a laden table at which we may sit with all of our preconceptions, questions, convictions, whims, prejudices and ideas – the few hundred readers (are there in fact as many as that?) may even disappear in this dinner party, and that would be an end to it. Such is criticism. At least the sort of criticism which gives the reader an appetite for the book.

For once we are all in agreement that such a feast is displayed for its many readers in the shape of the one hundred and twenty plates in this book. Yes, we wish this book – which is sparing only in words – countless friends. The silence of this researcher who presents pictures will win respect. Perhaps his learning is of the kind which strikes speechless any who possess it, and in this case technique is more important than knowledge. Anyone who accomplishes such things is endowed with more than just modest skills. He has produced a catalogue of minute observation and perception which will immeasurably change our view of the world. He has proved how right Moholy-Nagy, that pioneer of new photography, was when he said: "The limits of photography cannot yet be predicted. Everything to do with it is still so new that even initial exploration may yield strikingly creative results. Technical expertise is obviously the tool of the pioneer in this field. The illiterates of the future will be the people who know nothing of photography rather than those who are ignorant of the art of writing." Whether we speed up the growth of a plant by using time-lapse motion camera or enlarge it forty times, whichever of these we do, a whole gamut of new pictures meets our gaze in place of the single image we knew previously.

These pictures disclose an unsuspected wealth of forms and analogies which we never imagined existed in the plant world. Only photography is capable of revealing these because the veil drawn over these mysteries by our own indolence is only pulled back by means of multiple magnification. Nothing can demonstrate the pertinence of Blossfeldt's revelations better than a comparison with an earlier and highly individual approach – its proponent was Grandville, a man as misunderstood as he was esteemed.[1] In his *Fleurs Animées,* he showed the whole cosmos springing from the plant world. Blossfeldt approaches the matter from the opposite direction – he marks these seemingly pure products of Nature with the undeniable stigma of man. Grandville, this great forerunner of advertising technique, wielded one of its basic principles – pictorial sadism – with more skill than any other. But is it not extraordinary to see, on the other hand, another basic technique of advertising – enlargement to colossal size – used by Blossfeldt gently to undo the damage done by caricature?

These works are called 'The age–old forms of art' *(Urformen der Kunst)* – true enough. But what else are they than age-old forms of Nature too? Forms then which were never simply ideal *objets d'art* but which from the beginning were the original underlying forms appearing in successive cycles of creation.

---

1 Gérard Grandville (1803–1847) was a well known French caricaturist. The bizarre nature of images mark him as a precursor of Surrealism.

Even the most impassive observer would be thrilled to see that the enlargement of parts of plants visible to the eye could be as extraordinary as plant cells glimpsed through a microscope. When we remember that Klee and, even more, Kandinsky worked for so long on the elaboration of forms which only the intervention of the miscroscope could – brusquely and violently – reveal to us, we notice that these enlargements of plants also contain original stylistic forms *(Stilformen)*. In the crosier depicted by the fern, in the larkspur and in the blooms of saxifrage, we see forms reminiscent of the tracery in the rose windows of cathedrals. When we see these plants pushing their way out of crevices one senses a kind of Gothic purposefulness. In the greatly enlarged pictures of chestnut and maple shoots we see pillars taking on the form of horsetails and totems. The buds of the *Eisenhuf* unfold like the body of an inspired dancer. Every calyx, every leaf confronts us with pictorial essentials which range through all stages of creation: metamorphosis in Nature has the final word. These have developed from one of the deepest, most unfathomable forms of creation – from the mutation in which the element of genius has always resided – the collective creative power of Nature. This fertile mutation is diametrically opposed to human invention – the *natura non facit saltus* of the ancients. One is tempted to call it the feminine, organic principle of life – yielding – infinite – artful – ubiquitous.

We wander amongst these giant plants like Lilliputians. Their sweetness can only be truly experienced by such great artists as Goethe and Herder – by those with the spark of genius in their minds and eyes.

ART FORMS IN NATURE

Dustwrapper for Karl Blossfeldt *Art Forms in Nature* London, A. Zwemmer 1929

Paul Nash 1932

Photography and Modern Art

A review of Karl Blossfeldt, *Art Forms in Nature*

Comparisons, odious or doubtful, have been made frequently between art and photography. Only recently, with us at least, photography has come to be considered individually, apart from its recognized value as a medium for portraiture. Today we do not withold from it the title of an 'art in itself', although this concession necessarily contains some reservations. In a former article I gave an outline of the history of photography which showed something of the curious misconception arising from its practice as an art competitive with drawing or painting. Subsequent developments have dispelled such confusions, but it is doubtful whether the importance of photography as a complementary science has been fully realized.

In Professor Karl Blossfeldt's second volume of *Art Forms in Nature* we have an intensely interesting example of the peculiar power of the camera to discover formal beauty which ordinarily is hidden from the human eye. Professor Blossfeldt remarks in his foreword, 'Every sound expansion in the realm of art needs stimulation', and I am inclined to think that this aspect of his contribution is of greater value than the demonstration of the beauty of Nature which he hopes will arouse the 'Nature-sense' and 'stimulate observation of our own plant world'. For it is the camera eye directed by acute human perception which is responsible for these remarkable observations. Actually these important forms do not exist for our vision except by virtue of a mechanical scientific process.

Since the publication of Professor Blossfeldt's original series it has become the practice to find likenesses between his floral forms and examples of antique art in sculpture, iron and woodwork. One of the best of the Zwemmer Gallery exhibitions, so intelligently organized by Mr Robert Wellington, was that devoted to the original photographs of Professor Blossfeldt's second collection. Alongside the plates solid counterparts of the plant forms in wood, stone and iron showed the extraordinary similitude in design between the natural growths and the 'inventions' of art. Were these likenesses accidental? Are we to suppose that the old artists derived inspiration from minute examination of natural phenomena? Obviously, in certain cases, natural forms have supplied a *motif*, but in many it would have been impossible to detect the significance of natural design without the aid of a mechanical process. This is where the camera's 'eye' proves its incalculable power, but not as an archæological, botanical or merely curious discoverer of 'interesting' comparisons between art and nature; its importance lies, surely, in the wealth of matter it places at the disposal of the modern sculptor or painter, which may prove stimulating to what Professor Blossfeldt calls a sound expansion in the realm of art.

Mr Wilenski, in his admirable treatise on modern sculpture has touched upon this aspect in an ingenious argument against the sentimental conception of Nature, 'the Romantic notion of a wild, free, ragged "nature" ', and has reinforced his logic by reproductions from several of the Blossfeldt plant photographs, which are indisputable evidence of definite, sculptural order most un–wild and by no means ragged or 'free'. But although this idea is sympathetic to my interest in the subject, it does not embody the point I wish to insist upon, which is that the manifestations of modern photography not only support the statements of many so–called 'perverse' sculptors and painters, but run parallel to and, to a great degree, influence the course of modern art.

In England we are yet in the loose grasp of Impressionism, but, as I have pointed out from time to time, a growing desire for a more ordered, architectural form of sculpture and painting is making itself felt among the younger school of artists. As an example of this tendency, although in some respects his work contains a contradiction, the recent exhibition of Edward Burra's pictures at the Leicester Galleries was worth a far more careful study than it seems to have been given – at least to judge by the 'criticisms' of the Press. In addition, I would suggest that Burra's extraordinary fantasies, perhaps the most original in imagination of any contemporary English artist, owe something to his keen appreciation of the æsthetic of modern photography. In his passion for solid individual shapes rounded and stippled to a high degree of finish with intense concentration upon highlights, in a peculiar insistence upon isolated objects such as the furniture of cafes, or upon bottles, baskets and napkins, or such foods as fruit or hams to which he gives unusual prominence, articulating their forms with the keenest appreciation of their surface properties, or again in his use of foreshortening and other dramas of perspective; in the sum of these characteristics he seems to have employed, with persuasive intelligence, suggestions which photography may well have supplied. In some of his compositions Burra makes use of the expedient of *montage,* or designs his picture on the *montage* principle. This is another instance of photographic technique suggesting an idiom for the artist. These practices are common enough on the Continent where the expansion of the realm of art is natural and continuous and receives every encouragement even for unlikely experiment, but, alas! our own little realm is somewhat confined – a field of buttercups and daisies with Union Jacks fluttering at all four corners, where our painters must play the traditional game, encouraged or admonished by hearty journalists and sentimental pedagogues with megaphones. It is not surprising that the delightfully unconventional antics of Mr Burra have merely earned him a severe caution for his pains.

In conclusion, I should like to urge such photographers as we possess, within or outside the film industry, to extend the limits of their experiments. Stunt arrangements and chic portraiture is not enough. Fortunately, this has occurred to at least two talented people – John Havinden and Barbara Kerr-Seymer, who are beginning to make individual reputations; and anyone who has seen the brilliant series of photographs of Russia in Mr Robert Byron's exhibition at the Abdy Gallery will recognize an amateur of unusual distinction.

Werner Gräff 1929

Foreword to *Es kommt der neue Fotograf!*

The purpose of this book is to break down barriers, not create them. Useful though manuals of photography are, so long as they describe the technique of the negative and positive process, they are positively harmful when they set limits based on aesthetic or artistic rules as these are generally presented. The style of 'picture criticism' in specialized periodicals, and the majority of photographic exhibitions, show clearly the extraordinary influence of the maxims constantly impressed on the photographer: the pundits have succeeded in closely circumscribing the art of photography, and only seldom do photographers dare to overstep the bounds set by them. Rules that stem from bygone eras of painting are set up as iron laws, though they can easily be shown to be untenable.

Given the insistence on these rules, it is not surprising that industry has almost completely concentrated on the type of camera necessary for 'regular' pictures, and this again makes it harder for the photographer to stray from the preordained path. It is time, therefore, to make industry aware of modern needs.

In what follows we are only concerned with photographic technique in so far as it relates to equipment and methods for producing unusual photographs. This is not a book about the technical elements of the photographic art. The fact that unconventional photographs predominate should not be misunderstood: we have nothing against ordinary ones. In a great many cases, a successful shot of the ordinary kind will no doubt serve the purpose best. All we are concerned with is that it should not be regarded as the only right and possible one in every case. For it is equally certain that the most telling effect can sometimes be achieved with shots that are completely contrary to the 'rules of the art' and are therefore condemned by its official masters.

Right. We hope you are now convinced that you should treat with great suspicion, and refuse to accept, any kind of restriction on the way in which you take photographs. Rules based on painting cannot be applied to photography without further ado, and even in painting the rules in question are completely out of date.

Photography is a free, independent art. It must not be subjected to alien, antiquated laws, nor should it be enslaved to Nature (does this surprise you?).

We can of course use photography to produce as good a 'likeness' of nature as we please. But it is not, as one might suppose, the first purpose of photography to produce 'lifelike' pictures.

On the contrary, we are quite well aware of its shortcomings for this purpose – first and foremost, the fact that it is not in colour. There are many cases in which this makes it sadly inadequate, and it is greatly to be hoped that colour photography will soon advance from its present crudeness and garishness to a state of greater refinement. But let us meanwhile use photography as it is.

Have you noticed, on moonlit nights, how uncannily expressive black-and-white scenery can be? This is not just the effect of unfamiliarity. The shapes of hills, trees and stones speak a language of their own, which is all the more distinct when they are devoid of colour.

But, even though photographs are in black and white, how few of them convey this eloquent language to us!

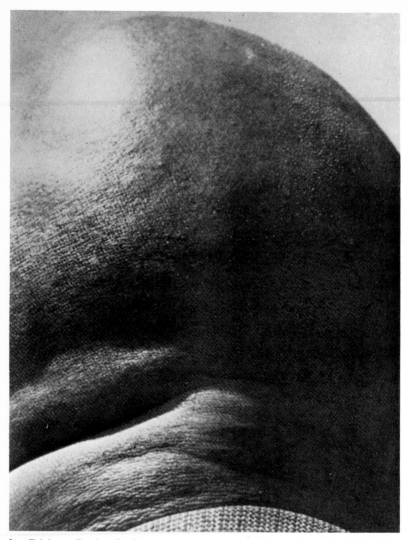

Lux Feininger, Dephot, Berlin

The reason is that they try to be too close to Nature. Yet one can make objects speak in any number of different ways by extracting fresh values from their forms.

The most impressive posters are made with the help of the new photography.

When will the postcard industry start to use its help? When shall we see the last of the usual boring 'scenes'?

A cautious beginning is being made with air and night photography, and there are already some photographic advertising cards.

Other developments will follow. This is a wide field for the photographer.

Finally, a word to equipment manufacturers, whose output must clearly be geared to the new requirements. First of all, the camera. The most frequent type, the baseboard camera, is essentially out of date. Apart from the baseboard folding camera it cannot be got ready for shooting quickly enough, and in any case it is too complicated. Although it is clearly meant for snapshots in the first instance, one scarcely ever finds a baseboard camera that lies in the hand well, especially for horizontal views. The industry should give up this type altogether and go over to new models. The development will certainly be in the direction of strut cameras and small cameras of the Leica type. However, cameras must also be better suited for work with a tripod than they are now. At present the assumption is that the photographer, after focussing on the ground-glass screen, can conveniently walk round the tripod to adjust the diaphragm, shutter, etc. However, the new photographer is often compelled by the nature of his work to crouch in an awkward position. He may, for instance, have climbed on to a cupboard or a makeshift platform on which he can scarcely move and certainly cannot get in front of the camera after sharp-focussing. The shutter knobs and aperture levers should be enlarged and provided with scales so that they can be conveniently operated from behind and from any position.

Tripods and tripod heads are a subject in themselves. Very few are as stable as they should be. The legs cannot always be fixed in the ground. Most tripods are designed on the assumption that the camera will be more or less horizontal; one has only to incline it slightly and the tripod slips. Ninety per cent of all tripod heads are useless or ill-designed. The requirements should be: complete stability in any position, allowing for inclining or elevating up to 90° in any direction, and maximum mobility in any direction even after the tripod and camera have been fixed to the tripod head. This last point has been especially neglected: it ought not to be necessary to move the whole tripod or loosen the camera in order to alter the view slightly. On the other hand the picture cannot be really composed unless the camera is fully mobile and can be secured in position instantaneously.

Optical manufacturers will have to give more attention to making cylindrical and other distorting supplementary lenses. These are by no means only useful for caricatures, but also serve to alter the values of natural features, street objects etc.

Finally, the trade should produce colour filter lenses for the transforming of tonal values. The manufacturer must carefully study the new photographer's methods if he is to supply equipment that will meet the new requirements.

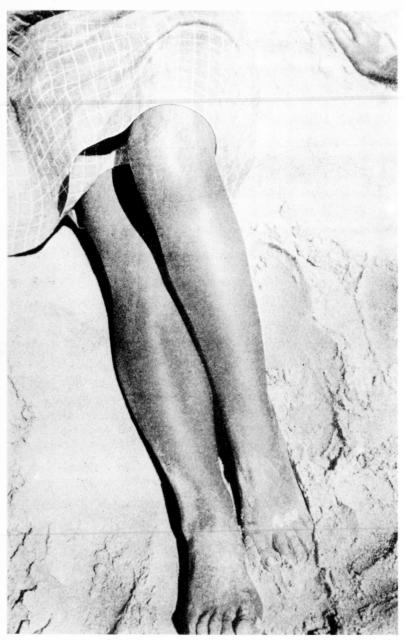

Herbert Bayer *Legs*

Franz Roh 1929

Mechanism and expression:
the essence and value of photography
Introduction to *foto-auge*

the history of photography hitherto shows two culminating periods. the first at the beginning of development (daguerre), the second at the end (see the photos of this volume and many 'anonymous' pictures published in illustrated papers). the greatest part of what has been produced between this beginning and end is questionable, because a frank or disguised attempt was made to imitate the charm that belongs either to painting or to graphic art. this of course was a deviation from the proper task of photography, a task which, though one cannot entirely escape the manner of seeing of his time and will always show a certain kinship to contemporaneous art, ought never to have sunk to imitation. the present bloom has not spread widely enough, for, after the misharvests of the nineteenth century, the ideals of visual formation in the broad public are still tainted. yet it may be taken for granted that true visual culture will expand more and more, and that (possibly in ten years already) we shall encounter as little semblance, pretence and bluff, as in mediaeval painting and graphic art, where no 'kitsch' is met with.

two circumstances are decisive whenever **cultural table-land** is to rise: in several places and at the same time single volcanoes must smoke, showering new pictorial ideas upon the land, sowing fertilizing lava. the existing soil must be of a kind to absorb and amalgamate manure. the supposition from above is already realized by single photographers such as appear in this book. the condition from below is also given: the appliances of new photographic technique are so simple that in principle **everybody** can handle them. the technique of graphic art (to keep comparison on the plane of black-and-white formation) was so complicated and slow, that up to the present time people were met with, who though absolutely possessing the visual power of forming, yet had neither leisure nor perseverance nor skill to learn the way of realization. the relation between conception and the medium of expression was too complicated. from this viewpoint it is characteristic that in this book non-professionals get a hearing. amateur signifies 'one who loves the thing', and dilettante means 'one who delights in the thing'. the german werkbund exhibition 'film and photo', 1929, this most important event in the visual field in the last few years, showed next to nothing by so-called **professional photographers,** who so often petrify in conventionality of manner. a renewed proof that rejuvenescence and elevation in various realms of life, of art, and also of scientific research, often proceed from **outsiders,** who remained impartial. thus this new bloom of photography also belongs largely to the field (now tilled by me) of misjudged history of general non-professional productivity.

the importance to the history of mankind of development of instruments such as the camera, lies in obtaining increasingly complex results while the handling of the apparatus becomes more and more simple. to maintain that 'short cuts' by relieving him of all effort, lead but to man's greater dullness and laziness, is romanticism in the minor key. the field of mental struggle is but changed to another place. the 'raphaels without hands' can now become productive. for it was likewise romanticism (this time in the major key), to assert that everyone who **has** something to say will find a way of saying it. only when the technical media have become so simple that everybody can learn to apply them, will they become a keyboard for the expression of many.

the statement is right, that not to be able to handle a camera will soon be looked upon as equal to illiteracy. I even believe that in schools the instruction in photography will soon be introduced in the **so-called** drawing lessons (while antiquated branches are dropped, let us hope). pedagogics – though of necessity coming after – always include in the programme of instruction the techniques that begin to become a general accomplishment of adults. in the days of charlemagne only the **scholar** could write, some centuries later all **cultivated** people mastered the technique, and still later every child. a similar process in a more limited space of time: in 1900 the typewriter was found only in remote special offices. today it is in use in all establishments, and tomorrow, meanwhile having become cheaper, every pupil will have one. whole classes of tiny children will drum in chorus on noiseless little typewriters.

the camera will likewise soon have passed those three typical stages. for it is not only the medium of wonderful pictorial **sport,** but has extremely practical backgrounds. today already the enormous increase of illustrated papers indicates how indirect view (written) is giving way to direct report (pictures of interesting incidents). thereby new possibilities take rise, not so much for draftsmen as for photographer-reporters in the broadest sense, at least for the grasping ones among them. whosoever in 1800 on a long journey wrote a diary of 300 pages, would in the present time take home 100 metres of leika-film-band that contain more complete memories than the word, being charged with contemplation. making use of the international language of outer enviroment that fundamentally neither changes after centuries nor after countries, the effect extends over a vast area of space and time. with regard to sociology it may be stated that photography serves the capitalistic upper classes by its steadily increasing insertion into advertisement. by a photograph we can gain a more accurate notion of the articles offered than by ever so suggestive a drawing. on the other hand the camera supplies a want of the lower classes: for we often meet a common man on a sunday excursion attempting to fix an incident of his holiday experience. all the more important is it therefore, that books providing a good horizontal section of the best results of the time should come to the masses.

from reporting in the broadest sense, as one of the main provinces of human craving for life, such pictorial preparation should be severed as aims at producing a **surface imbued with expression.** here some mis-instructed people still raise the question, whether – in principle – to produce a photo full of expression and finished to the very corners can be an impelling inner necessity. what we mean is the question whether we are – exclusively in this sense – concerned here with **art.** commonplace men and 'connoisseurs', both of whom generally are misforms of existence, still often meet in refusing to the most finished of photographs the quality mark of 'art'. either there is here but the semblance of a problem, since the definition of art is wholly time-bound, arbitrary and ungreat, or human sight is totally deformed and susceptible only to one kind of beauty even opposite nature. if however we understand art as an end in itself, called forth by man and filled with 'expression', good photographs are included. yet should art be understood but as manual production expressed **by the human hand** under guidance of the mind (what would be unwise indeed), we can establish a new category without diminishing the aesthetic value of these forms. it is a grave, subjectivist error to believe that forms pervaded by the aesthetic arise exclusively when every line has sprung from the 'smelting-pot of the soul', i.e. the mind-guided hand of man himself. of the three vast realms of all expressive appearance the above limiting definition would contain but **one.** neither aesthetic perfection of certain forms in **nature,** nor of certain **machines** likewise not created for expression, would be possible.

in this book we encounter forms quite coming up to the above definition; that in fact establishes but one rate, one **quality.** they are the photos in which we wish nothing to be moved, raised or levelled, no part to be either materialized or dematerialized, &c. there surely are people who will declare of even the **best** of photos that they do not reach graphic art in power of expression. yet that this is not a question of **photography** can be demonstrated, in as much as the very same people usually also refuse new painting and new graphic art, whether it be abstract, constructivist, or objectivist art. whosoever finds the photographs in this book, for instance, far-fetched in section, stiff and unorganic (I have met such people), generally has the same reproach ready for painting and graphic of the younger generation. sufficient proof that this has nothing at all to do with a special problem of 'photography and mechanism', but rather with the new, tenser, and more constructive seeing.

photography is not mere **print** from nature, for it is (mechanically) a turning of all colour value, and even of depth in space, and structure in form. nevertheless the worth of photography lies in the aesthetic value of nature itself. is it but necessary to master the implements of photography to become a good photographer? by no means: as in other fields of expression personality is required. the peculiar human valuation of form at the time is expressed in the photo just as it is in graphic art. to all probability – of course for the trained eye only – the locating of anonymous photos as to period and country is only more difficult **in degree** than locating works of graphic art, painting and sculpture. and this even when the contents of a photograph (costume or the like) cannot be dated or located, and there are but a series of landscapes or of animals to compare.

this **individual constant quality** that, as in the arts, is remarkably lasting, suffices to show that a good **photo** is also based on an organizing, individualizing principle. it often occurs that photographs taken by the **one** will always appear uninteresting, though he be skilled in technique, while photos by the **other,** who considers himself but an amateur and whose work is not technically perfect, yet invariably are of forcible effect. contrary to graphic art the principle of organization in photography does not lie in all-ruling manual re-forming of any bit of reality, but in the act of selecting an in every way fruitful fragment of that reality. if in the graphic arts there are a thousand forms of **recasting and reducing** the exterior world, there are a hundred possibilities of **focus, section and lighting** in photography, and above all in the **choice** of the object.

this **limited** range of possibilities permits of realizing significant individualization. we generally overrate the number of the few elements required to obtain ingenious forms. what a simple and confined instrument is the piano (to change to another field) with its ever-returning octave. and yet by constantly changing combination of the given elements, every pianist can draw forth a world of his own from these few series of tones.

the choice of the object is already a creative action. 'tell me with whom you associate and I shall tell you who you are' is a saying applicable also to the section of reality before which we stop. as distinctive as it is of a man what women move him, so characteristic is it of the photographer before which forms he stands spellbound, which focal angles and springs of light enthrall him. how organizing the general principle of photography can act at times is indicated by the fact that the diltheynohl doctrine of types, applicable only to psychically conditioned formations, may be applied, particularly if the index of period is added, thus stating that since about 1920 **all** types have a dash of so-called duality tension.

our book does not only mean to say 'the world is beautiful', but also: the world is exciting, cruel and weird. therefore pictures were included that might shock aesthetes who stand aloof. there are five kinds of applied photography:

the reality-photo, the photogram, photomontage, photo with etching or painting, and photos in connection with typography.

the **photogram** hovers excitingly between abstract geometrical tracery and the echo of objects. in this tension there often is a peculiar charm. these pictures, as is known, are taken without a camera, only by the meeting of certain objects with sensitive paper. by exposing them a long or short time, holding them close or far, letting sharp or subdued artificial light shine upon them, schemes of luminosity are obtained that so change the colour, outline and moulding of objects as to make them lose body and appear but a lustrous strange world and abstraction. while going from snowiest white, across thousands of shades of grey, down to the deepest black the most transparent tone degrees are gained, and by intersection and convergence an optic semblance of space that can suggest the most distance as well as plastic closeness. as with all human systems of disposition, it is at first difficult to 'calculate' the effect of objects while still in the process of taking them, yet gradually one acquires a feeling for the result. in the beginning there are often but chance hits. it is however a noted error on the part of idealistic subjectivism to conjecture that fully expressive effects cannot be called forth in this manner. it is a question of rejecting a number of pictures. in art (as in etching for instance) the process of selection lies largely in the mentally remodelling hand (I), in photography (reality-photo) it lies in stealing upon the most suitable bit provided by environment (II). whereas in the photogram selection lies **at first** in eliminating failures – for according to the law of **probability** a stroke of luck will occur sometimes (III). constant practice and a good 'instinctive disposition' will soon move the process from the third sphere to the second. with such advance a crescendo of value in all forming processes of life will be gained, and in the **quantity** of successful attempts, but not in the order of the three kinds of possible perfect hits.

just as the making of silhouettes was very popular a hundred years ago, so the photogram will become an ingenious pastime of the present day. it is far superior to the silhouette, for it permits of a thousand gradations in shade between black and white. by this means not only the intersections and disclosures mentioned above are possible, but actual penetrating of bodies, whereby the covered part remains visible and the whole charm-system of transparencies can become effective. it is however by the sublime possibilities of gradation between the poles black and white that polyphony of tones is obtainable.

new attractions have also been added to the **reality-photo.** in the first place new objects have been drawn into the sphere of fixation, a furtherance of the process. for man in the jog-trot of sensual life generally conceives but a conventional impression, and rarely actually experiences the object. thus I remember how some people, otherwise quick at grasping, would not make allowance for the taking of the paris sewerage canal, until those very same people finally arrived at understanding how expressive and almost symbolic such fragments of reality can become.

next to a new world of objects we find **the old seen anew.** here the difference in degree of intensifying plasticity becomes a pictorial means. for a long time we had photographers who clad everything in twilight (imitators of rembrandt in velvet cap, or all softening impressionist minds). today everything is **brought out clearly.** yet herein recipes are not admitted, and occasionally the palpably plastic may be put next to the optically flowing, whereby new effects are gained in pictures which the narrow intellect of the professional is inclined to point to as failures.

'wrong' focalizing, so-called mistakes in the scale of distance, sometimes will, if ingeniously used, provide new optical attractions, as also the use of the same plate over again (photographs one in another). a further means: new view in the

Hans Finsler *Incandescent lamp*

way of **perspective.** formerly pictures were taken only in horizontal view-line. the audacious sight from above and below, which new technical achievement has brought about by sudden change of level (lift, aeroplane, &c.) has not been utilized sufficiently for pictorial purposes so far. new photos show this up and down of appearance. here the taking of a vertical line (standing house, mast, or the like) obliquely, is stirring. the significance lies in opening astronomic perspectives so to say: vertical in this greater sense really is radial position corresponding to an imaginary centre of the earth.

comparatively new is also a further variety of the reality-photo: the **negative** print. the principle of **inversion** is known in arrangement of abstract forms, as applied in weaving and wicker-work. it occurs in music too, though seldom. why should not the same principle be applied to exterior realities though they be not in ranges? besides the inversion of **direction** an inversion of light-and-dark is well possible. this, for the present, specifically **photographic** charm cannot be experienced elsewhere, for the distinction between **a day and night view of the same reality** is quite a different thing. we might perhaps speak of a world in the major and the minor key, to indicate at least the completely changed expression of tone values.

there is furthermore the **combination of photography with graphic art or painting** to point to, of which examples are given (see max ernst's marvellous works). to maintain that here is a mingling of **heterogeneous elements** that can never combine is but an empty doctrine.

remains the **photomontage** (produced by cutting, pasting and mounting). this form took rise from futurism and dadaism, and has gradually been clarified and simplified. photomontage, formerly a demolishment of form, a chaotic whirl of blown up total appearance, now shows systematic construction and an almost classic moderation and calm. how flexible, transparent and delicate is the play of forms in 'leda', and crystal-hard the starry miniature world of dadamerica. the fanciful of this whole species is not factorial fantasticality, as was a certain stage of cubism, where the simple world of objects was dissected into complicating structure, but an **object-**fantasticality in which from simple fragments of reality a more complex unit is piled up. it was significant that here the principle of mosaic, that so far had been applied only to particles of colour and form, was to such an extent applied to parts of the objects themselves. though these possibilities of formation are met by the technique of photography, yet 'montage' is based on a deep need of human imagination. this is shown not only in futurist pictures, but also in irish twisted ribbons, in the copulation of objects on romanesque capitals, and particularly in the paintings by bosch and bruegel, where most extraordinary forming fancy expresses itself fully in such graftings of reality. a new and rich pictorial humour is rising here. no wonder that many people think comic papers of the future will make use of this resource. it is of no moment that they still hesitate to do so, for some score years ago they let **draftsmen** of new style wait long enough too.[1]

the use of photomontage for advertisements has already spread considerably, and also for outer book wraps (that appear so much more alive than the heavy, humdrum cloth covers they so mercifully conceal). the malik verlag has been leading in productions of this kind (and that at a very early date). in spite of the humour, or the merely advertising character, of these things, they should not be looked upon as trifles, or only incidental details, for they can be of demonic-fantastic effect.

we now reach the last class, the interesting **combination of photograph and type,** of which we show important specimens. we have little to say here, as these things speak for themselves and have found an extensive field in the advertizing business.

the most important utilization of photography, the cinema – a marvel that has become a matter of course and yet remains a lasting marvel – is not within the province of this book. we are concerned but with the statically fixed, with situations that merely pretend dynamic, while in the cinema, by **addition** of static situations, real dynamic rises. questions of form here enter an entirely new dimension.

---

1. georges grosz writes to me: 'yes! you are right. heartfield and I had already in 1915 made interesting photo-pasting montage-experiments. at the time we founded the grosz & heartfield concern (Südende 1915). the name "monteur" I invented for heartfield, who invariably went about in an old blue suit, and whose work in our joint affair was much like the work of mounting.'

A. Kraszna-Krausz 1929

Exhibition in Stuttgart, June 1929, and its Effects

Extract from a review of the *Film und Foto* exhibition

Though not a film-exhibition *par excellence*, but in the first respect a very intensive collection of modern photography (and in connection with it the regular performances of the work done till now by those young and detached ones, who call themselves within and beyond the frontier the Avant-garde), the spectator was won by the sympathetic endeavours of *Herrn Gustav Stotz,* commercial leader of the *Württembergische Arbeitsgemeinschaft des Deutschen Werkbundes* to whom the whole thanked its existence.

Not only because of its importance the photographic exhibition must be remembered, but also, and principally because of the valuable recognitions by which the Stuttgart photographs led to conclusions for films.

From Germany, England, France, Holland, Austria, Russia, Switzerland, Czechoslovakia, and the United States one saw the collected work of those who assert themselves to belong to photographic production that is consciously modern. Before one reached the pictures grouped after their original countries and personalities, one went through a room created by *Prof. L. Moholy-Nagy* that represented the development since Daguerre and the spheres of scientific, reporting and advertising photography, in large, distinct lines; the final conclusion of the whole is that the task of photography of today is to devote its specific technical means to the active service of the present time, by immediate unembelished, catching of true impressions of life.

The truth of this sentence can then be tested by examples given in the exhibition, in an interesting way. It becomes clearly apparent, that the most characteristic and strongest impression is given by pictures that unveiledly aim at a certain purpose (as the photos of material by *Paul Outerbridge*, New York; the photos of fashion by *George de Hoyningen-Huene*, Paris) – or by those pictures that give an unfaked reproduction of situations (war photos of the *Reichsarchiv Potsdam*; criminal photos of the *Württembergisches Polizeipräsidium*, Stuttgart) – that vitally catch physiognomies (women's photos by *Otto Umbehr*, Berlin; mens' photos by *Helmar Lerski*, Berlin) – immediately discovered objects (photos of architecture by *Renger-Patzsch*, Harzburg; animal photos by *Hedda Walter*, Berlin; flower photos by *Imogen Cunningham*, California; photos of oysters by *Edward Weston*, California).

But everywhere, where one had got too far distant from the purpose, and approached the artistic modification of the object (portrait photography by *Cecil Beaton,* London) – where the decorative treatment is in the foreground (material photos by *Hans Finsler*, Halle) where original perspectives are sought for but for their own value (genre photographs by *L. Moholy-Nagy*, Berlin) – where black-and-white contrasts are noisily elaborated (photos of scenery by *Sascha Stone*, Berlin) – where an intermediate state becomes the function of a result in an original way (negative photos by *Andreas Feininger*, Dessau) – where the interest for the object is replaced by shrewd composition (abstract photos by *Francis Bruguière*, London) – where optic distortions reach for laughable effects (caricature photos by *Werner Gräff*, Berlin) – where scraps of pictures are cut and made up for a unit (photo-cuttings by *Hanna Höch*, The Hague) – where absract lights on the plate attempt to substitute concrete ideas (photogramms by *Man Ray*, Paris) – there, yes, there the new photography

Exhibition poster, Berlin 1929

distinguishes itself from the old one only by a trick, that bluffs today as well as it will be surpassed tomorrow. If one rises immediately against 'anti-compositions' that treat lines, against decorative still-lifes, and impressionistic landscapes, if one stands up against manual procedures, technical tricks and plays of art–craft, one must not forget that photogramms, photocutting and modified optical drawings move in the same sphere.

It is fascinating to witness the crystallization of young technical methods at first, for they are always a sign of development and so also of liveliness. It is also instructive to watch how these must die off, if they are overbred as an expression of themselves, instead of finding the way to lasting contents by supression of their own. The expression, technics, is civilization, life of the body and consequently mortal. The contents, the art, is culture, life of the soul and so perhaps immortal.

Oswell Blakeston 1930

A review of Franz Roh and Jan Tschichold, *foto-auge*

In the days of Charlemagne, says the author, only the scholar could write; today, every child can write, tomorrow, will everyone be able to take a photograph?Will camera classes replace antiquated drawing lessons? Will the man who cannot handle his camera be branded as an illiterate?

The author goes on to point out that those people who find photography "far-fetched in section, stiff and unorganic" have the same reproach ready for the graphic arts of the moderns.

The illustrations cover the usual ground; usual in these beautifully produced German books, but still revolutionary in England. Florence Henri, with her strip of mirror and crystal globes; El Lissitzky, with his bottle of paste; Max Ernst, with painting on photographic backgrounds; Moholy-Nagy, with a Paris drain; Peterhans, with the bits of everything that make up still life (death?). They are all very clever, and, I suppose, they have to go on – one with the mirror and globes, the other with the bottle of paste – for fear they should not be functioning on the tremendous day when England becomes alive to the world beyond the walls of The Royal Photographic Society.

Plate 73 is a police record of a man murdered with violence.

"Next slide, please," as the lecturers say.

Florence Henri *Composition — Cottonreels* 1928

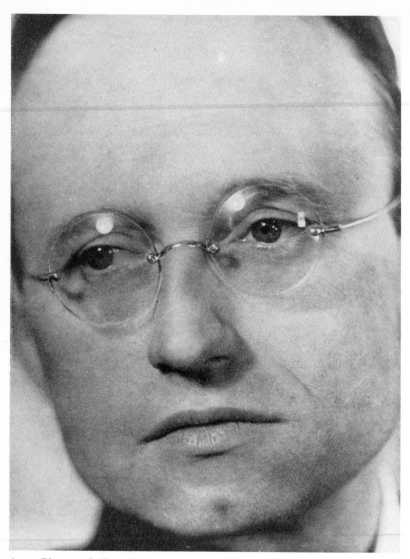

Aenne Biermann *Dr Franz Roh*

Franz Roh 1930

The literary dispute about photography
Theses and antitheses to the theme
'Mechanism and expression'

Introduction to *Aenne Biermann:* Fototek 2

Of the following wrong objections none is feigned. All have been either printed or written. I cannot *prove* my counter theses here, but shall do so in a chapter of my book *Prejudices of the Present*. To provide a plane from which to compare art and photography, always liken the photo to *graphic* art each time recur to a plane in black and white.

Leipziger Anzeiger 1839
'To hold fast evanescent mirrored images is not only impossible, as has turned out after thorough German investigation, but the mere desire alone, the will to do so, is blasphemy. Man was created in the image of God, and no man-made machine can hold fast the image of God. Should God abandon his eternal principles and allow a Frenchman in Paris to give to the world an invention of the devil?'

> *H. Brockhaus 1839:* 'The invention of Daguerre is one of the most interesting which has ever been made.'
> *Jules Janin in Paris 1838:* 'Never has drawing by the greatest master produced anything similar.'
> *Schopenhauer 1851:* 'Daguerre's invention is a hundred times more ingenious than Leverrier's much admired discovery of the planet Uranus by means of calculation.'

The photograph does not tell the truth.

> After all *naturally* not. The arrangement of the lenses will include a degree of subjective taste of the period (in the Gothic period they would have been arranged for verticality and compression of depth.) And also the instrument as such will hardly become quite perfect. But in many ways it already is superior to the human eye. For the time being there is no possibility of optically seizing the external objects more truly. Even the colour-photograph, which at present is still intolerable, is but a question of time. And the great possibilities of the *cinema*, too, derive from the fundamentals of photography.

Photography as a mechanism of mere reproduction kills the creative in us, and becomes a menace to art.

> By this mechanism the creative is but pushed to another place. The act of choosing the object, the section, the lighting, the gradation of depth, the degree of sharpness, the paper, &c., all this combined, provides an although limited, yet broad enough scale of freedom in facing nature.

The possibilities of liberty as compared with the graphic art, for instance, are so limited and so firmly established, that they cannot suffice to produce forms full of expression.

> Mankind generally overrates the *limited* number of possibilities of liberty and established means required to make individualization and real formation feasible. (Example given from quite another zone: how simple and firmly established an instrument is the piano with its ever-repeated octaves, and yet how much individualizing formation is possible here.)

39

Photography is a splendid means of reporting. In this alone lies its task. Truly artistic
people look upon photography rather sceptically.

The whole controversy of the present, whether one should report or
form freely, has nothing to do with photography in the first place. It is
altogether a fundamental dispute, lying at the root of formation, and,
moreover, it is to some extent only a semblance of a problem. The
photograph, too, contains *both* possibilities. Though it most frequently
functions as a report, it can become an absolutely aesthetic aim in
itself, *just like all man-made form in general.* That truly artistic persons
appreciate the photograph exclusively as a *report,* is not right. We
quote two *painters* of the foremost ranks: Man Ray, (Paris) and
Moholy, (Berlin.) They were the ones to assert the claim of photography as a self-aim. There are now photographers, whose work by far
surpasses graphic and other art, both in unity and in detailed finish of
surface.

This notwithstanding, photography is not art.

That depends only on how the concept art is defined. If under art only
purely manual production is understood, a new category can be established for photography. But if, on the other hand, art is understood to
be nothing else but fully expressive, self-purposed form called forth by
man, good photographs must be included.

By propagating photography, one helps to lower and level the mental plane. Photography
is at its best 'applied art', and certainly but the intellectual ground floor.

Perfectly wrong! *Photography* can as well run through all the steps of
the ladder, from the most trivial to the highest rung.

A photograph cannot, in a deeper sense, express the individuality of its producer.

In significant photos one can determine the individual-constant in the
outlook on life as well as one can in a graphic work, although quite a
different process of production is dealt with. A 'phenomenalogy of the
act of *choice*' would already suffice to explain this 'mystery' intima-
tions on this subject in my treatise. 'Mechanism and Expression' in
'Photo-Eye', Stuttgart 1929. In the meanwhile confirmed philosophi-
cally in Springorum's substantial book *'The Object of the photograph',*
Munich 1930.

While in art all particulars remain immutably in their place, they can be changed even in the
good photo.

As a matter of course also in the *photo* — if it is good – all is necessary
and immutable. That this is attained in quite a different way in the
photo (and is even occasionally but a chance hit), does not in the least
speak against the structure of the result.

In photos things have but value as a remembrance, they have no value in themselves, as in
art.

Stands good at most only for the reporting photo, and even then not
always.

Modern photography is not spontaneous, it has similarity to modern painting and sculpture, and thus works by rejecting and not by distinctly formulating.

What opponents *praise* in the former ages (the similarity of structure in
sculpture, painting, graphic and architecture, as for instance in Gothic
art) they *find fault* within the present (typical cultural snobbery.) Yet
as long as mankind will live, formations of the same periods will show
the same structure, even when produced by widely different techni-

ques. Yet the fact that many photographers produce the relation in a way not pertinent to the matter, must not be passed over in silence.

Really important objects are seldom photographed nowadays, but puddles, eggs, buttons, spools of thread, and the like. Every object should be of importance in itself.

An objection often right in particular cases. Yet fundamentally, as it is intended, this objection likewise proves wrong. It finds acceptance only for the reporting photo. Namely, if a 'section of a puddle close by' appears as expressive as the 'Atlantic Ocean from an airplane view', it is the puddle which – from the point of functional vitality – is to be preferred. Because it shows us optical significance in places that are usually overlooked by conventional people. (The world can become optically significant *everywhere.)*

It is the contemplator, who, so to say, puts value into the photograph, while the value contained in a graphic work comes forth toward us.

What naïveté in theory of cognition! Here again genesis and result are confounded.

The effect of art is unequivocal, the photograph remains ambiguous.

The effect of art is also ambiguous. Let an auditory describe one and the same painting, or let one and the same person describe the same painting in different months.

The photograph can never express real materiality.

Every true judge of the development in history of art although this objection comes from so-called connoisseurs will sense the concept of 'materiality' here as being absolutely conditioned by the period of substance-naturalism or impressionism, according to which a Dürer even has no 'materiality' in his drawings (as has been said.)

Individualists of 1930 shudder at the thought that everybody will soon photograph.

The same shudder people might have felt about 1630 at the thought that soon everybody would learn to write, and thereby hold fast their experience, instead of this being reserved for those exclusively, who have things of importance to say. With great calmness history passes over such resentment.

The keen photo-joy is already out of date. It is stopped by its own pioneers. The big photo exhibition of 1930 in Munich, for instance, is like the Glaspalast there: an immense wholesale stock of good and bad.

Initiators will always stop when their central movement broadens. Never in history has a stone, fallen into the water, let itself be prevented from drawing ever wider circles. Photography particularly should be placed in the line of collective activities, as should all that can be obtained by instruments which function easily. The question of exhibition and publicity will also settle. First the initiators appear, who are often of high quality (yet by no means *always* in history). Then broader exhibitions follow the superjoy of new expansion. And then, as a matter of course, indifference toward secondary photos will rise, and sifting will become doubly severe. To speak of photo-inflation is as justified and as unjustified today, as if formerly a writing and printing inflation had been spoken of. In such cases the sound man always will think collectively, and protect himself in *quite a different* manner against lowering of level.

Aenne Biermann *Double Photo*

Oswell Blakeston 1931

Recapitulation

A review of Franz Roh's *Fototek* series

A number of portrait photographers, of prodigious reputation, would soon be forced to admit defeat if they were ever so foolish as to undertake to produce 'artistic' close-ups with a motion picture camera. Their work is not really photography for they spend hours with the lead pencil building up the faces of their models. In fact they go to the length of taking negatives which will supply a mere framework.

Those who complain about these deft practices are generally the jealous ones. After all, money, in immense quantities, can be made from the game: the sitters are so happy to find that a man can be persuaded, by any means, to say such flattering things about their faces. The mischief is done when these portrait painters begin to influence the younger photographers. For the sake of the rising generation we believe the wielders of the lead pencil should be denied the title of photographers and given that of artists!

Talented Moholy-Nagy is one of those who is a little weak on his technique. He has made films, but we have never seen them. However, we saw his work in *Malerie, Fotographie, Film* and now in the first volume of the new *Fototek* series (Klinkhardt and Biermann, Berlin). He is good at pasteage and photograms, yet he hardly deserves the magnificent translations of the captions . . . 'Geometrizing clairobscure strukture.' 'Photographic immediacy of the instant.' 'Dematerialized house.' 'Degrees of plasticity, of darkness and of abstraction.' . . . Moholy-Nagy (with or without pencil) cannot compete with this superb translator of the original German. He faces a photo with its negative. He pastes (we like our word pasteage) up long shots and close-ups, adding a few lines to accentuate perspective. No: the translator IS the star of the book.

The second volume of the series is devoted to Aenne Biermann. Franz Roh contributes a long preface on *The Literary Dispute about Photography*. He reminds the reader that people objected to the photos of Daguerre as inventions of the devil (any ink to sling at photography)! And he discusses the objection that, as photography has similarity to modern painting and sculpture, the camera worker REJECTS instead of FORMULATES.

Aenne Biermann believes in real photos. She attempts to make ordinary objects look interesting: a lobster claw, hot water bottles, broken egg with reflection. Like Moholy she faces a large eye open with a large eye shut. Nevertheless, she has technique. The agate magnified forty nine fold is changed (unlike apples on a plate) to interest by the lens of the camera. There is a nice double print of a piano and strings. There are: the possessive chimpanzee with his arm round the girl; the conifer branch; the man and woman lying on the beach. The translator is less obtrusive.

The make-up of both volumes is by Jan Tschichold.

Other books in the series will be 'consecrated' to: El Lissitzky, Police Photos, Photomontage, Kitsch Photos, Sport Photos, Erotic and Sexual Photos.

G.P. (Berlin) *Flags, at the State exhibition, Berlin* October 1931

Max Dortu c.1930

Come before the Camera

'You must all come before my camera:
Honourable gentlemen with close-cropped hair,
Veterans of student duels,
You must all come before my camera:
Ladies in automobiles,
I want to take aim at your high breasts,
You must all come before my camera:
I capture you with my flashlight,
All you champagne-drinking parasites,
And I want the rest before my camera too:
The hospital with its suffering and distress,
The screams of women in childbirth,
And then the final picture in my camera:
Flags of victory all over the world,
And human beings holding one another's hands.'

Preis 30 Pfg.
V. Jahrg. Nr. 9

Der Arbeiter-Fotograf

BERLIN, SEPTEMBER 1931
NEUER DEUTSCHER VERLAG

OFFIZIELLES ORGAN DER VEREINIGUNG DER ARBEITER-FOTOGRAFEN DEUTSCHLANDS

AUS DEM INHALT:

Bild-Wort-Montage / Wahl der Platten und Filme / Zustandsfotografie
Ultrafoto / Wir und das Recht / Bilderkritik / Büchermarkt / Tausch-
ecke / Ortsgruppenberichte / Geschäftliches

DER HERR

F. P., Breslau

Cover of *Der Arbeiter-Fotograf* September 1931

Edwin Hoernle 1930

The Working Man's Eye

From *Der Arbeiter-Fotograf*

'Another Bolshevik exaggeration!' I hear the reader exclaim. 'Surely the eye is essentially the same organ in all human beings, and only illness or injury can alter its structure and functions. Of course it varies in different animal species – spiders, bees, snakes, cats, elephants – but as far as human beings are concerned we cannot speak of workers having one sort of eye and industrialists, ministers, bankers and lawyers having another. Marxists and Leninists should really keep their feet on the ground a bit more!'

Not so fast, my dear fellow-photographer! Even your example of the industrialist, minister or banker shows you to be wrong. If a German factory-owner goes to America, what do you think he sees? The Ford works at Detroit, the Chicago slaughter-houses, Standard Oil derricks, the White House, Fifth Avenue; but do you think his eye, the eye of a keen German business man gorged with profits and eager for more – do you think it sees the six million starving unemployed, the human wrecks at the Ford works who are not yet forty years old, the tiny anaemic children worked to death at seven years of age in the textile and canned goods factories of that most democratic and Christian country, the material and spiritual misery in the negro quarters of the notorious lynch-state of Texas, or the blood-thirsty brutalities perpetrated on striking workers by the bought, bribed police force in the streets and factories? And if he should come across them once in a way – for he cannot always be blind to the seamy side of American 'freedom' and 'prosperity for ever' – he still doesn't actually see them, because there is a block between his retina and his brain: the pictures taken by his 'natural' camera, the one in his head, are not developed and do not reach his consciousness. Or, if by chance they should ever reach the mind of this worthy business man, absorbed in his calculations of profits and high living, they are neither clear-cut nor properly lit – they remain minor exceptions, small shadows in the picture-collection of his brain and his camera, if he has one or the other about him. And even a bourgeois reporter who goes to America or – to compare small things with great – to a wedding in Berlin for the express purpose of filming 'the people', will not encounter genuine types, for all his sharp eyes, or, if he does, he will not dare or understand how to photograph them without retouching.

What is essential is psychological vision, the liaison between the physical retina and the picture that arises in the minds eye. How little the average person is trained to perceive facts is something we can observe any day in ourselves or our neighbours. Can we estimate distances correctly? The word 'estimate' itself shows that we do not feel certain. Five minutes after looking at a house-front, can we remember what its features were? We may take the same city walk every day, but how many of us notice what a splendid theme that wretched little newspaper-seller would be for our proletarian camera, or what an insolent criminal-looking type that member of the Hitler Youth is whom we pass regularly in the street and who perhaps will one day shoot down one of our best friends under the benevolent eye of the democratic police? One needs the professional eye to pick up at once certain details of landscape or machinery, the clothing or habits of other people; and you need the eye of a certain class in order to perceive the signs of prevailing social conditions in the internal and external life of our fellow-beings, in the structure and appearance of homes and factories, their internal organization and the general picture of life in the streets, or even the shape and size of fields and meadows and the crops grown on them.

What is more, this 'proletarian eye' must be trained. Millions still lack it altogether, and others only have it imperfectly. Only a very few have the practice and discipline to exercise their class vision at all times and places, on holiday, at weekends and on journeys, at leisure as well as at work. The rule for the working-class camera-man should be: No camera without a proletarian eye behind it!

Almost all bourgeois pictures, whether 'artistic' or vulgar, reflect the cult of leisure and idleness. This is represented in the theatre and films, in illustrated papers and novels, in newspaper reports and commercial advertisements; and when the proletarian and his girl go to 'have their picture taken' they choose a more or less elegant leisured pose like that of a clerk in the firm of Tietz or the wife of Krupp's general manager. Only the quality of the execution varies according to the sitter's purse and his degree of education. And if the proletarian gets himself a camera on hire-purchase, in nine cases out of ten he will start off, exactly like his bourgeois neighbour, by snapping some 'beautiful view' or 'romantic nook', a family party or a pretty girl, in short something as remote as possible from the class struggle – for what he wants in his album are 'pleasant memories' that will help him to forget the sordid misery of everyday life. At best he may aspire to art photography: a handsome nude, an artistically viewed landscape. And he really thinks he has achieved 'revolutionary art' if he photographs a completely naked body or a smoking factory chimney instead of the

Tina Modotti (Mexico) *We are building a new world* 1930

usual half- or quarter-clad damsel or landscape of mountains, rivers or the sea. But here too the proletarian photographer must learn not to stop half-way. We are not Philistines, whether it is a matter of culture or the revolution. We take pleasure in the sight of a pretty girl, in real life or in photography, in contemplating mountains or the sea or the peaceful charm of a meadowed valley. Why not? – but this is not the deciding factor. A handsome face, an imposing tree, a lizard sunning itself on a rock – naturally these too are proper subjects for a proletarian camera; but they are not the subjects that distinguish us from the cultivated bourgeois who tomorrow, perhaps, will sentence our fellow-workers to prison or lead a gang of Nazi thugs against us, and whose fine education and first-class camera are paid for by our sweat and our childrens tuberculosis.

This is the gulf, this is where our world begins, this is where our proletarian eye should start to function; and only from this point on have we the right to call ourselves worker-photographers.

The workers' world is invisible to the bourgeoisie, and unfortunately to most proletarians also. If the bourgeoisie depicts proletarians and their world of suffering, it is only to provide a contrast, a dark background to set off the glories of bourgeois 'culture', 'humanity', 'arts and sciences' and so forth, so that sensitive folk can enjoy a feeling of sympathy and 'compassion' or else take pride in the consciousness of their own superiority. Our photographers must tear down this façade. We must proclaim proletarian reality in all its disgusting ugliness, with its indictment of society and its demand for revenge. We will have no veils, no retouching, no aestheticism; we must present things as they are, in a hard, merciless light. We must take photographs wherever proletarian life is at its hardest and the bourgeoisie at its most corrupt; and we shall increase the fighting power of our class in so far as our pictures show class consciousness, mass consciousness, discipline, solidarity, a spirit of aggression and revenge. Photography is a weapon; so is technology, so is art! Our world-view is militant Marxism, not mere academic wisdom. And we worker-photographers have an important sector of the front to hold: we are the eye of the working class, and it is we who must teach our fellow-workers how to see.

Tina Modotti (Mexico) *Peasants fight with us!* 1930

Willi Münzenberg 1931

Tasks and Objectives

From *Der Arbeiter-Fotograf*

Photography has become an outstanding and indispensable means of propaganda in the revolutionary class struggle.

Thirty or forty years ago, the bourgeoisie already understood that a photograph affects the onlooker in a very special way. If a book contains pictures it is easier to read and more likely to be bought, and an illustrated magazine is more entertaining than a leading article in a political daily. Photography works upon the human eye; what is seen is reflected in the brain without the need for complicated thought. In this way the bourgeoisie takes advantage of the mental indolence of the masses and does good business as well, since the illustrated papers often achieve a circulation of millions.

Not only that, however – much more important is the ultimate political effect produced by a combination of several pictures, with their captions and accompanying texts. That is the decisive point. In this way a skilful editor can reverse the significance of any photograph and influence a reader who lacks political sophistication in any direction he chooses.

The revolutionary workers of all countries must clearly understand these facts. They must fight the class enemy with every weapon and defeat him on all fronts. Just as the Soviet workers have learnt to make their own machine-tools, to devise inventions and use them in the service of peaceful socialist construction, and just as workers in capitalist countries have learnt to write their own newspapers, in the same way proletarian amateur photographers must learn to master the camera and use it properly in the service of the international class struggle.

The history of the organized workers' photography movement does not go back a long way. Just on five years ago a dozen comrades got together in Hamburg to form the first local group. Six months later the first number of our journal, *Der Arbeiter-Fotograf,* appeared; it then ran to eight pages. In April 1927 the first country-wide conference took place at Erfurt; there the Association of German Worker Photographers was founded, and the first exhibition of proletarian photographs was held. To the comrades who sent us their pictures in those days we can now say: 'You were pioneers, your powerful work made a tremendous impression, your pictures aroused enthusiasm throughout Germany'.

In these five short years we have managed to build up an organization which today numbers over 2,412 members in 96 branches and produces a newspaper with a circulation of over 7,000. The revolutionary workers' press no longer depends on bourgeois photograph agencies; our worker photographers have learned to focus on the right objectives, to produce social documentaries, to organize political exhibitions and illustrated lectures.

In the past year we have advanced a good deal further. Our tasks are limitless: we have a world to conquer, and our own world to defend. We have, through delegates, made contact with comrades in the Soviet Union; on the 30th anniversary of the Revolution we sent five workers who travelled all over Russia and, on their return, described to numerous meetings in Germany the magnificent successes and endeavours to fulfil the five-year plan in under four years. Their enthusiastic reports were far more effective than any in the past, because these comrades had at their disposal 80 photographs which they themselves had taken and which bore witness to the truth of what they had to tell.

We are now strong enough to take an even bigger leap forward. The task before us is to broaden the attack against international capitalist exploitation. We must move forward, rally the world of proletarian photographers in all countries, give them a policy and tasks to perform. We already have well-established groups and associations in America, France, Holland, Scandinavia, Czechoslovakia, Switzerland, Austria, Rumania and Japan. These groups are still weak, but they exist and are prepared to fight shoulder to shoulder with us. So we have decided, in agreement with comrades in other lands, to set up an International Bureau of the Association of Worker Photographers of all countries.

You will have read our appeal in the last issue of *Der Arbeiter-Fotograf.* Since then we have decided to hold our first international conference in conjunction with the Tenth Congress of Workers' International Relief in Berlin at the beginning of October. A large international exhibition of photographs will be part of the conference.

Our most important task in the next six months will be to prepare for the conference and exhibition so that they may have the maximum political and organizational effect in all the main capitalist countries. In this connection the International Bureau will have the following tasks:

1. To organize further groups and associations and see that they receive political guidance and technical training.

2. To correspond intensively and make personal contact with actual and potential working-class photographers in all important countries.

3. To put the different branches in touch with one another and especially to develop links between the German and the Soviet branch.

4. To prescribe specific tasks for each country and propose themes for treatment in preparation for the international exhibition.

5. To organize competitions between different branches.

6. To hold an international week in July under the title 'Proletarian Photography'.

7. To draft an international programme of action and Statutes for the Association.

That, in broad lines, is our programme, and we must now mobilize all our forces. In the next few weeks we need ten portfolios of photographs for the different branches. And we shall do our level best to create a living international movement.

For proletarian photography, the output of class-conscious members of the working class, must play its part in protecting the work of Soviet socialist construction against attack by the imperialist gangsters. It must help to spur on the workers and peasants of all countries to destroy the capitalist system and establish the rule of all workers and the dictatorship of the proletariat.

Collective work is our strength

Our branches are turning away more and more from the traditional modes of operation. They are beginning to realize that severe economic difficulties, unemployment and chronic shortage of money are not insuperable obstacles if they are met in the right way.

Several officials have discussed this matter in letters to our journal, and we give here a summary of their ideas. We also particularly ask technicians and group leaders to keep us informed of their efforts and successes in this line.

Most local groups possess dark-rooms for the use of all their members. Sacrifices are made to create, enlarge and administer new working premises.

Thus a basis for collective work already exists, and our next task is to make it fruitful by systematically developing the resources of local groups. Working evenings of the whole local association are replaced by contacts between individual groups, meeting and working at different times in accordance with their character and special tasks.

Comrades are assigned to their respective groups at a general meeting of members, so that each collective consists of four or five members. The number of collectives and the formulation of their tasks depend on local conditions and the size and composition of each local association.

Each collective is assigned special tasks by the executive of local associations and by the whole membership. The ablest and most energetic comrades should be put in charge of the collective. They are responsible for the thorough training of their group; they should apportion and direct the work and report on it at least once a month to the general assembly. The technician in each local group must instruct those responsible and must of course be in close touch with all working groups. He must be closely informed of their work, its progress and any setbacks, in order that he can intervene personally in case of need.

Besides collectives for the young, for beginners, and other special groups corresponding to local circumstances, special care should be devoted to forming and looking after collectives for the unemployed. There is probably no local group in Germany that does not suffer from the fact that some of its members are out of a job. This does not mean that they should remain idle. They must be kept in the ranks of those fighting against starvation and misery, thanks to the solidarity of their comrades still at work, who must entrust them with the tasks they are best able to perform. It should not be necessary to show in detail that there are many such tasks, for the unemployed are well provided with something that workers generally lack, and for the want of which they cannot achieve important objects – namely time. They must no longer waste their precious leisure on more or less idle pastimes. It must be our first duty to prevent the unemployed becoming lazy and indifferent. With our meagre resources we can do nothing to help them economically, but we can help them to remain active as worker photographers by letting them have equipment free of charge. After the whole collective has received a thorough basic training, definite tasks can be assigned: preparation of sets of photographs, travel series, reportage and so on; the treasury of the local group must look after finance for the time being. There must be a careful check that the best use is made of the materials provided and of the finished product. With help from workers' newspapers and local proletarian sport and educational organizations, the work can be made to pay for itself and not impose a permanent burden on local funds. The unemployed should also be used more than hitherto for organizational work, especially for seeing that subscriptions are paid up fully and on time. Another source of income that has hardly been exploited as yet is the organization of sales of *Der Arbeiter-Fotograf.*

August Sander *Secretary (Cologne)* 1931

Alfred Döblin 1929

About Faces, Portraits and their Reality

Introduction to August Sander, *Antlitz der Zeit*

I   Is the Individual Real, or What is Real?
There was a famous controversy among scholars in the Middle Ages. It happened a thousand years ago. The disputants called themselves the Nominalists and the Realists. It is certain that this controversy is still continuing today though under a different name. Today it is difficult to say in one sentence what it was all about a thousand years ago, for meanwhile words have changed their meaning considerably; however, I will try to give you some understanding of the tactical situation: The Nominalists were of the opinion that only particular things have substantial reality and exist; however, the Realists maintained that only the universals, let us say, the genus, the idea has substantial reality and exists. What has this got to do with faces and portraits? I can soon show you. And now let us talk about two kinds of levelling; the levelling of faces through death and the levelling by society and its class structure. What do I mean by levelling? Every man becomes equal, personal and private differences are wiped out. Differences disappear under the stamp of a greater power, thus, the two forces, death and class.

II   The Levelling of Faces Through Death
Some time ago a young woman was pulled out of the River Seine. The stranger, who had undoubtedly committed suicide, was brought to the Paris mortuary and there she soon attracted attention. I will soon tell you why. A death mask was taken from the 'stranger from the Seine' (l'inconnue de la Seine). Many people have a reproduction or a cast of this mask. What was so striking about the young stranger and what makes so many people want the prints or casts of the mask? I will try to describe the head. It is the face of a young woman or girl maybe 20 to 22 years old. She has straight hair parted in the middle. One cannot see the eyes, the eyes cannot see, this girl is dead. The last thing her eyes saw was the bank of the Seine and the water of the Seine. Then these eyes closed, and then came the short, cold fright and the giddiness. Suffocation and insensibility came rapidly upon her. But it did not stop at that. I would not think that the girl went gladly into the Seine. What came after the initial despair and the brief horror of suffocation we can now see from the mask. It was reflected in her face, and therefore she was not simply put aside like the hundreds of others in this mortuary. The stranger's mouth is slightly drawn in, the lips are almost pursed and so the cheeks follow suit. Now below the peacefully closed eyes – they are closed from the cold water and also to see only an inner vision. Below these eyes, round the mouth a really sweet smile develops, not a smile of bliss or ecstasy, but a smile that is calling and whispering and perceiving something that is familiar. The stranger approaches bliss. There is incidentally an uncanny allurement and temptation in this face and in the way the mask reproduces it. And even if there is a certain reassurance in the thought of death, this face, however, exudes something which is almost infatuating and alluring.

What about this interpretation? We come back to what I mentioned before, the levelling of the human face through death. There are collections of death-masks and a book of such a collection is before me. And when one turns over the leaves – the lovely stranger is also there. A great uniformity becomes obvious, the faces are certainly different, Wieland's face is certainly different from that of Frederick the Great, Jonathan Swift or Oliver Cromwell's moustached, strong-willed face or Lorenzo Medici's voluptuous, broad face. Some faces appear to be in the full bloom of health, others are worn out by long illnesses. But all these faces have something negative in common: something has been taken away from all these men. They have not simply closed their eyes giving them the image of the non-living or maybe of just being asleep. Not only has death stilled all animation but somehow has erased all individual presence. But what remains of the face? The result of life-long work and life's work on the flesh and bones, on the contours of the features, on the shape of the forehead, nose and lips. These remaining faces portrayed in the death-masks, their expressions are the stones which have been rolled and polished by the sea washing on them for decades. And no longer a single instantaneous movement is kept and preserved. What I have in front of me is the end result. Now work is over. What called for a halt and levelled all these faces and made them uniform, death. Two great processes made them individuals and personalities in life: they were moulded by their race and the development of their personal ability – and through the environment and society which promoted and hindered their development. But now nothing promotes or hinders them any longer – the eyes are rightly closed, as no further life emanates from these men any more. And the feeling one gets about the dead is that they are not only silent and complete in themselves but that they are less, they are objects in other hands. They were active: that formed their faces. Now they endure something, they are passive, a cast has been taken from them. Death as something positive. For a while this used to be Hugo Wolf, Dante, Fox, Frederick the Great – now they are all conquered, satisfied, quiet objects. The basis of life remains. But the lovely stranger from the Seine is smiling? Yes, there is a strong influence coming from this new anonymous power. Not everybody allows himself to be carried away from here easily. At best many fall asleep, or, when they enter the anonymous realm of Death a gentle sleep comes over them. But some of them do come near to a kind of happiness. Their individual life has only mistreated them and hindered them. Now these obstacles have been taken away from them. Now, since their eyes have been closed on this individual existence they can welcome with a smile, another, a different level of existence which is unknown to us; they can pursue their life full of sweet expectation, full of longing.

III   The Levelling of Faces Through the Class Structure

There is another folder in front of me with portraits of living people. These have not yet fallen into the big tub where their individuality and all activity have been washed off them. The water that polishes these stones can still be seen on them. They are still rolling in the sea which rocks us all. And while the death-masks communicate the same overwhelming anonymity – we see into a great and strange moonscape – here we look at individuals. Odd! One should think that one is looking at individuals. But suddenly one notices that even here one does not see any individuals. Admittedly it is not the great monotonous moonscape of death whose light falls on all the faces; it is something else. What is it? We are talking now about the astonishing levelling of faces and portraits through class structure, through the level of civilization. This is the second levelling or assimilating anonymity. To use the word from the mediaeval controversy I mentioned at the beginning: we have seen how effective the universal Death is. It proves a real power (and force): yet it does not say what it really is, the Scytheman or the lovely bringer of peace. And now looking at the portraits, the living, we are confronted with a second universal which proves to be real and effective and powerful: we are confronted with the collective power of human society, the class structure, the level of civilization.

IV   Particulars from this Group

Every one of us knows a number of people and we recognize them by certain quite personal characteristics. One only meets individuals, and each person has his name and also his particular and characteristic signs which are unique. It is hardly necessary to mention the thumb-print; as the criminologists know, this can really only be a fact, relating to one particular person, by which this person can be identified. I maintain that this 'forensic' thumb-print is not necessary. For us other things in life can be sufficient, things less strict and numerically precise, which, however, have sufficient exactness. We see a man, his height, his posture, his face – a wealth of complex visual information, but we comprehend in one glance. There is this characteristic voice, this gait, this gesture, and already we have enough for us to be always absolutely certain of identifying this man and to identify means to recognize him as a unique being. And his uniqueness is quite self-evident to us.

But what do we say about an ant-heap? There are perhaps about 500 ants on their way from a root, or some stones, moving quickly and apparently randomly. A hundred paces away an even larger crowd is working – even if we watched these small creatures very carefully we would never get further than noticing certain characteristics of the species and insignificant differences between the individual insects. Here it is absolutely impossible to differentiate. And yet there is no doubt – at least I would imagine so – that all the creatures know each other and can distinguish between each other: as is probably the same with the bees. What am I aiming at? At something quite familiar but seldom applied to humans, that is: at a certain distance the individual ceases to exist and only the universals apply. The individual and society (or the universe) – (Oh, Solomonic situation) – a matter of distance. As we are humans we are only dealing with individuals – among humans. With coloured people, however, we certainly find it more difficult. If we were elephants in the zoo, we would divide humans into those who just go past and those who give us sugar. The keepers would form their own group, a particular species of humans. However, there are enormous advantages in observing human beings, that is us, in that way. It is not necessary to have an elephant's point of view, maybe, or an historical philosophical or economic point of view might be sufficient. Suddenly we become strangers to ourselves and have learned something about ourselves. It is of immense value to learn something about oneself. Whether one makes use of it is another matter all together, but just to have the knowledge is valuable. Our pictures here are concerned with the widening of our field of vision. I shall soon show you. We have some beautiful teaching material in front of us.

V   There are Three Groups of Photographs

I cannot find that the photographic lens sees any differently from the human eye. Maybe, it sees less well as it is fixed, however, what the lens shows us is the same as we can see for ourselves. Contrary to our retina the plate behind the lens can record an image, and the photographers make different use of these images; they use them for different purposes. This is the photographer's decision, however, the photographer like the painter can teach us to see certain things or to see in a certain way.

There are photographers who see artistically and for whom the face is only material for a picture. They seek effects of an aesthetic kind. Those pictures are called 'very interesting' or 'very nice' or 'original'. These are also values, but at least you cannot learn anything from them about human beings or about yourself.

Then there are photographers who flourish in every town and village, though there are so many of them they mean more to us than those 'artistic gentlemen'. They want to give as great a 'likeness' as possible of the people who pose in front of them. The photograph should be as like as 'possible', that is, the personality, the individuality, the uniqueness of this human being should be recorded on the plate. Let us go back a little and let us remember our introduction: these photographers of likenesses, they are the Nominalists who have no knowledge of the great universals. I suppose we do these gentlemen too much honour when we say they have taken their position in the great controversy of the intellects and they have decided to side with the Nominalists. The existence of a certain realism is undisputable among this group of photographers, that of making money. And then we come to the third group. I have not counted the pages or sentences I have spoken so far; but we can hoist a flag now; we are at the point now, our photographs! You know already how it is with this third group of photographers – here is me boasting about a whole group however, there certainly are but very few; in Germany, I have only met Sander – this third group belongs consciously to the followers of Realism. They think that the great universals have substantial reality and lo and behold! when they take a photograph it is not a likeness, so that without any doubt and quite easily you can recognize Mr X and Mrs Y. What you recognize, however, and you should recognize – I shall tell you in the next paragraph.

VI   What these Photographs Should Tell You

This essay is like a huge balloon which is carrying a small gondola. However, there is little more I have to say. The truth has been prepared, and now a philosopher (Sander) is following me. The photographs, the expressions of this philosopher, each speak for themselves and together in their order they speak more elegantly than I can do.

You have in front of you a kind of cultural history, better, sociology of the last 30 years. How to write sociology without writing, but presenting photographs instead, photographs of faces and not national costumes, this is what the photographer accomplished with his eyes, his mind, his observation, his knowledge and last but not least his considerable photographic ability. Only through studying comparative anatomy can we come to an understanding of nature and the history of the internal organs. In the same way this photographer has practised comparative photography and therefore found a scientific point of view beyond the conventional photographer. It is up to us to read the varous interpretations of his photographs; on the whole the photographs are superb material for the cultural, class and economic history of the last 30 years.

There are the rural types who are likely to remain as their form of small holding, which has remained stable for a long time. So today this group has not disappeared or become extinct – only their importance has been lessened. You find with them the united families; even without the plough and field you can see that the work these people are doing is rough, hard and monotonous; this kind of work makes their faces hard, makes them become weather-beaten. When new conditions come they change, wealth and easier work makes the faces soften.

Let us pass on to the types of the small town, then to the closely related types of the suburban craftsmen and compare them with the modern industrialist. Let us go on to the photographs of today's urban proletariat. It gives us a quick summary of the economic development during the last decades. We must not ignore the remaining images if we are to understand in what way this development has progressed, the figures from the Workers Council, the anarchists and the revolutionaries. Men are shaped by their livelihood, the air and light they move in, the work they do or do not do, and moreover, the special ideology of their class. A glance at the pictures in group 3, the Bourgeoisie and their children, can teach us more than lengthy reports or accusing references. The tensions of our time become obvious when you compare the photographs of the students who must earn their living with the professor and his bourgeois family; who seem very composed, feathered in satisfaction and still without misgivings.

The rapid change of moral attitude during the last decades is illustrated through group 4. There is still a group 4 to mention. The Protestant vicar, a marvellous photograph; he is surrounded by his pupils but the expressions on their faces no longer accord with that of their teacher and his gown. The village schoolmaster walks about in the country with his beard and spectacles, strict and sober, a conscientious idealist. The 'corps student' wears his little cap, he has duelling scars across his face and feels the splendour of his sash. The composed wholesale merchant and his wife belong to this group; these are pictures from 'Debit and Credit'. These are not the modern tycoons but behind them other new types are already visible. The class structure is undergoing a revolution, the cities have grown enormously, some originals are still there but new types are already developing. So this is today's young merchant, this is the pupil from the grammar school; who would have thought it possible 20 years ago, the way the characteristics of age have mixed, the way the youth is marching on. And this pupil from a girls' secondary school dressed in the fashion of today's young ladies; she is already a young woman. The divisions between youth and adulthood have become less clear, the dominance of youth, the urge for rejuvenation and for renewal which even has biological effects has become obvious. Whole stories could be told about quite a lot of these photographs; they invite us to do so. They are material for authors, which is more stimulating and yielding more than many newspaper reports.

These are my suggestions. He who knows how to look will be enlightened more effectively than through lectures and theories. Through these clear and conclusive photographs he will discover something of himself and others.

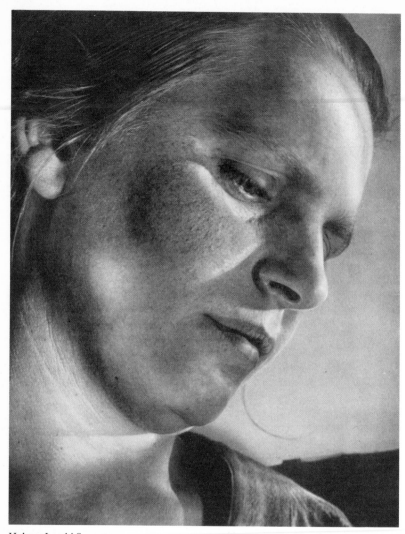

Helmar Lerski *Seamstress*

Curt Glaser 1931

Introduction to Helmar Lerski, *Köpfe des Alltags*

A book which seeks to arouse the reader's sympathetic interest in photographs of unknown human beings for no reason but their optical or, to be more specific, their aesthetic qualities must face the initial question whether and to what extent photography is entitled to advance a claim that appears to put it on a level with the fine arts. This in turn raises the basic question of the meaning and nature of photography, to which very different answers have been given at different times. Certainly the inventors and first users of the new technique believed it to be capable of replacing, once and for all, the work of the human hand: the machine age, they were convinced, had evolved an instrument which was destined to liberate pictorial art from its roots in craftsmanship.

There is no need to waste much argument on this naïve error, for the results of painting and those of photography are as unlike as sunshine and electric light. But, just as sunshine and lamplight both serve the purpose of illumination, so photography and graphic art have many essential points in common. Both of them project a three-dimensional object on to a flat surface, both convert tonal values into light effects, and both can be used to make representations of people and things. In this last respect photography has held its own *vis-à-vis* graphic art; it has shown itself capable of taking over functions which could previously be performed only by the artist's hand. But it does not follow from this that photography has taken its place on a footing of equality with the other arts. On the contrary, a development which did not become widespread until after the invention of photography seemed calculated to set very strict bounds to the claim of the new technique to be regarded as an art medium. We are not suggesting that photography was the sole or principal motive force of this development. But even the most passionate art-worshipper need not fear to admit that the incursion of photography into the sanctified realm of painting has left visible traces in art history. Photography supplanted the portrait-painter, the painter of townscapes and the reporter who used his pencil to depict current events or travel scenes. But, once released from the objective task of portraying objects and events, the artist was all the more free to proclaim the law of subjectivity which has governed all new developments in painting since the victory of Impressionism.

By forcing the artist to withdraw to the impregnable position in which he was free to follow his own bent at the expense of 'likeness' and 'representation', photography made even clearer the limits of its own penetration into the sanctum of art.

The idea of a boundary fixed for all time, however, does not fully answer the old question of the nature and possibilities of photography. Even if machine-made and hand-made pictures can never be measured by a single standard, this does not mean that photography can have no aesthetic merits. Apart from any comparison with graphic art, we may enquire whether photography cannot be an art in its own way: not only in the sense of technical mastery or perfection (as *techne* is simply the Greek word for 'art'), but also in so far as art contains a personal, conscious, subjective element, raising it above the level of a craft.

For a long time photographers, in their ambition, misunderstood this requirement: they tried to compete with painting on its own ground and to achieve similar effects by technical means. They thought they could bring photography closer to art by imitating the latter, and believed they had achieved their aim when they managed, by photographic methods, to reproduce painterly effects such as were popular in the age of Impressionism.

At that time the contradictory notion of 'art photography' was evolved. It was considered 'artistic' to select views in such a way that the composition came closest to the Impressionist ideal. In so far as the camera's unswerving objectivity might seem an embarassment at a time when subjective art was at a premium, attempts were made to counteract this by blurring the negative with an 'atmospheric' effect or applying intricate copying processes to the positive, giving it somewhat the appearance of a chalk drawing.

The pointlessness of trying to erase the frontiers in this way is nowadays universally recognized. 'Art' photography has fallen into disrepute. The question of the aesthetic possibilities of photography had to be posed all over again, not only because the fine arts had meanwhile given up those painterly effects that photographers had copied from them, but especially because technique had developed on its own lines, regardless of aesthetic deviations, and had pointed the way back to photographic effects which had been appropriate from the beginning. It turned out, in fact, that the important role of photography in the field of science and reportage was more conducive to impressive visual developments than were petty attempts to imitate the fine arts. The serious work of designers and inventors went into perfecting technical equipment for microphotography and instaneous shots, which proved to have more to do with progress than the painful efforts of amateurs to compete with graphic artists on their own ground.

Modern equipment has made photography so easy that it really requires no special skill or talent to produce a satisfactory or even a pleasing picture. Technique has advanced to the point where it can dispense with the human hand or even the human mind, by devising an apparatus that takes several pictures, in quick succession, of an object that has only to be left in readiness at a given spot. The Photomaton process denotes the victory of the machine and apparently, therefore, the final proof that photography and art are two different things.

But this is not really so. For although the world-spanning task of pictorial reporting, including pictures of individuals, is more or less automatic from the technical point of view, requiring little more than prescence of mind and determination on the reporter's part, the photographer is still free to perfect his handiwork in the same way as the artist who used to perform the reporting function. The modern photographer no longer needs to imitate alien effects to give his work the status of an art: he knows more about the intrinsic possibilities of his own technique.

Photography no longer competes with graphic art – their provinces are clearly separate – but it can itself become an art in so far as it is consciously made use of by the human spirit and creative will.

The modern portrait photographer, like the portrait painter of former times, is confronted with the problem of 'likeness', but it does not present itself as the central issue. In both cases the artist no longer believes in the literal reproduction of objective fact, since an object can only be presented analogically on a flat surface. The modern photographer, like the painter, realizes that a true portrait must express his own opinion of the sitter's nature.

A transformation is in prospect when photography, as an art, seeks to distinguish itself from a craft that is on the point of turning into an industry. After almost a hundred years photography has returned to its starting-point by divesting itself of all the doubtful aids of sophisticated printing processes. The photographer no longer aspires to be a painter; light is the medium in and by which he seeks to create. He wishes, by his own proper technique alone, to produce pictures that bear witness to the spirit and hand of man, who makes his equipment an obedient instrument of his will.

The following pages reproduce works by a photographic artist who conceives his mission in this way. Helmar Lerski believes that the photographer's medium cannot by its nature be anything but light. He uses light to model the features of a human face, to make it speak in a particular way. He works with mirrors that reflect sunbeams, and he uses shadows to draw sharp lines on a face, to make furrows and hollows; he allows light to play upon salient forms so that the whole surface becomes lively and the expressive, plastic image of a human countenance comes into view.

In photography of this kind the model is only raw material, to be shaped by the artist's creative will. It has been boldly suggested that all possibilities are contained in every human face, that it is only a matter of seeing them and making them visible to others. We have made a consistent effort to substantiate this idea, and anyone who scans the reproductions in this book will see how the photographer has succeeded in infinitely varying what might seem to be unchangeable features. Take, for instance, one of the many individuals who once lived in prosperity, who were impoverished by the war and inflation and had to adopt a humble calling. The photographer sees their downfall and represents it in a succession of pictures, making the light first quiet and gentle, then hard and glaring; the outlines are softer or sharper, the camera aimed so that the head appears to be erect or lowered. This is a drama of light in which the subject himself plays no part: he does not have to adopt a certain pose or visual expression. He sits quietly, and because he has to sit for a long time, as the procedure is complicated and the exposure must be lengthy, his features relax into the neutral state that enables the photographer to give them the expression he feels to be appropriate.

People whom no one knows and who do not know themselves are the best subjects for this new, special type of photography. Those who play a significant part in life or on the stage, what are nowadays called 'personalities', wear a mask when they come before the camera. They know how they wish to appear, and they do not like to leave themselves in the photographer's hands. Just as Russian film directors came to the conclusion that ordinary townsfolk and peasants were more suitable for their purposes than famous actors, so Lerski uses as models people encountered in the street or hired from the labour exchange – believing as he does that everyone has a face, only one must make the effort to see it.

Photographic art is now sovereign in its own sphere, and determines its own purposes and tasks. Just as painters at a certain stage gave up portraits of well-known people and began to paint studies of unknown ones, so as to be valued for themselves and not because of the importance of their sitters, in the same way the photographs in this volume are not of celebrities but, as a matter of deliberate choice, portray the features of ordinary people. Beggars and the unemployed, hawkers and street–sweepers, washerwomen and housemaids – all of them sat for two hours in front of Lerski's camera and left behind them images of human misery and greatness, displaying a wealth of expression and unsuspected psychological depths. The street-sweeper, for instance, never in all his life dared to hold his head upright; but the camera does it for him, and his profile is one that a dictator might envy. The washerwoman knows that her features are hard and bony; but the light makes them beautiful, and the lens gives her a noble, pure expression. The beggar – as the camera looks at him from different angles, and the sunlight plays on one feature or another – becomes a versatile actor, playing a new role in each photograph. The young workman, as a flickering gleam lights up his profile, is like a character from a revolutionary drama.

None of these know anything of the parts they are playing, and they do not care about a likeness, as their own appearance is unkown to them.

Lerski's technical methods are based on using the utmost possibilities of his equipment. The picture produced on the focussing screen by the artist's choice of viewpoint and lighting is fixed on the plate with the maximum sharpness and accuracy. Nothing is concealed or added, nothing blurred or beautified. The lens moves so close that the pores of the skin appear as if under a magnifying glass, and the subject's head is often too large for even the biggest plate: part of the chin or skull must be sacrificed, but this only concentrates the effect by enhancing the expression of the eyes, mouth and nose.

Others have produced photographic still-lives by similar methods. The camera's explorations, which have ranged all over the world and into the remotest fields, have finally taken notice of the insignificant and the near at hand. There is no doubt that these studies too have an optical effect of their own, and it would be wrong to dispute the charm of a well-ordered composition in black and white. But their originality is limited to the selection and arrangement of objects and the choice of a projection plane.

Lerski's heads, too, are carefully composed in terms of tonal values; their outlines are deliberately planned and they fill the space compactly. They are aimed at aesthetic effect, although their peculiar genre does not compete with any kind of painterly or graphic art. Thus they are not 'artistic' photographs, but they display photography as an art, producing pictures which thrill us and increase our visual knowledge – pictures which seem to lay bare the soul by displaying its creator's intention, and which exert an aesthetic effect in their gradations of light and shadow and their two-dimensional use of black and white.

These pictures may be called poor likenesses, as they contain more subjective expression than objective statement. But we have for a long time been misled by the claim of photography to be 'objective'. Since painters took to portraying unknown models and thereby freed themselves from the duty of producing a likeness as it had previously been conceived, they came to understand portrait-painting in a new and deeper fashion and to take a different view of what resemblance to the original really consisted of. In the same way it appears that Lerski, by his experiments, has thrown a new light on the art of portrait photography, which up to now has shown surprisingly little readiness to take advantage of modern developments in photographic technique.

Kenneth Macpherson 1931

As Is

A review of Helmar Lerski, *Köpfe des Alltags*

Of a recent German book of portraits, a Berlin critic complained that a washer-woman looked like an aristocrat: that by selecting the angle at which the face, the camera and the light should be placed, the faces could be, and had been, transformed to the whim of the artist.

Life is strange indeed: many have extolled the 'one' virtue of cinema – of the film camera – as being a possibility (if not a facility) of effecting certain emphases or stresses which give an illusion of transformation, of 'moulding' objects to a more subjective or unconscious inference.

This, in the way of common talk, is sufficiently true for everyday use; nevertheless not wholly true. A human brain can construe the material, the objective in many ways, not excluding the ghostly and the hoped-for. Indeed, the ghostly and the hoped-for (and the feared) are often soley 'real', and life 'as such' – as rule-o'-thumb routine – takes either second place or no place at all.

Reality – a catchphrase – could hardly be otherwise. As human flesh and blood is commonly considered 'more real' than the skeleton beneath, certainly more real than the 'soul', the 'spirit' and those other starry definitions for the unconscious; so by the very law of paradox which plays so rampantly with our lives, the expression 'flesh and blood' has grown to mean a kind of allegory, something mystic – as, in fact, Humanity, with a capital H, transcends in sentiment and sentimentality its sole constituent – people, with a small and insignificant p.

With cinema, what is true is not that the camera or the 'director's intention' or both, can be responsible for the references signalled to this or that member of an ultimate audience, but that the references are created solely within this or that member of the audience – not collectively (though collective emotional response is a force of which we must be constantly aware, and do our best to harness if we will) but as varying degrees of reciprocation in individuals. What is significant to one will pass unnoticed by another. The director and cameraman may aim at definite responsive stimulus, on the assumption of which they build their plan, they can calculate and estimate – and nowhere better than in a film of masses – infection of mass hypnotism and auto-intoxication. But a similar aim will be less certain of successful achievement in films where implication is the principal tension – 'suspense', for example has a more or less established formula, as have the other cinematic stimuli – 'romance', 'pathos', 'violence', 'fear', and so on.

But with the increase in subtlety, objectivism is gradually replaced by symbolism; one is embarking on an expedition where experts only can be of use. As I see film, the coastal fringes have been examined, paddled in, bathed in; piers have been built, casinos and bandstands, there are the well-known promenades, there are urban district councils and their by-laws – which some of us would willingly, alas, make immutable already! There is something neat and respectable about it, having 'toyed' so much with big ideas, it reminds me rather of Mrs Rosita Forbes and her 'pilgrimages'. But what I do see as the valid province and territory of film is an unexplored one, a few bold pioneers have cut a way into the hinterland, a few more have gone out in frail craft on uncharted seas. Film has a tinkle-tinkle about it, which sometimes comes over one in waves; it has skirted

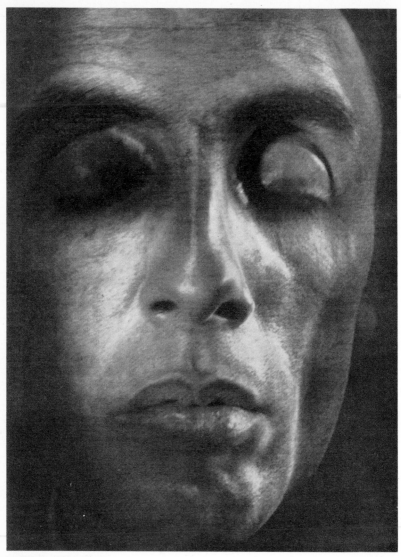

Helmar Lerski *Journalist*

its own reality. It is full of assumption and swank, but underneath knows well enough the kind of ignoramus it is, doling out casual fondants.

Where films have stood their ground, where they have been strong enough to look away from their invalid's esplanade, they have been like falling stars, solitary and indicative only in so far as they perhaps excited interest among those who might have desired to follow them. By all this talk I mean that there has been too much chit-chat about art and sociology – and not enough quiet engineering. You could take the theme of the film *Turksib* as an example of the kind of organization and purpose which should go to opening arterial roads for the film; and as an example of exactly the kind of doggedness which it has never known. You could take the article by Eisenstein in this issue as the blue print of a future highway. It is the forward drive that is so difficult. you do some dynamiting, levelling; it seems stupendous. But usually it is only another area – a site – which has been made; to become swiftly a parade–ground.

It is impossible for the director to say 'I have done this, and those who see the film will feel this and this'. In its most complete form the film can be but an *index*: that is its true function.

The greater part of a film is that which takes place, not on the screen, but in the mind of the beholder.

And it can be quite externalized and in narrative form, as, for example, a news-reel record of the Prince of Wales arriving or embarking somewhere. In a London West End theatre this event, not in itself overwhelmingly exciting, and often very badly photographed, will beyond all else provoke a torrent of applause. Other countries, with the possible exception of the Dominions, for which I am unable to answer, find no pulse set in agitated commotion by the event, and if a lone pair of hands starts clapping in the dark, you will know they belong to a Britisher. I remember when Graf Zeppelin was first brought out, I saw a film of it in a Berlin Palast. Deutschland uber Alles was struck up by the band, and instantly a transfigured audience pressed entrancedly to its feet, and when it was all over went on applauding in a transport. It was very moving.

There seems to be a superstition, however, that people and objects have an aspect which alone is real; one aspect and one only. That if a camera tilted cunningly, or a face compellingly lighted makes 'a washerwoman look like an aristocrat', then the cameraman is *altmodisch,* he is suffering from a decadent and played out traditionalism.

One has to ask oneself, and then anyone else who will listen: What is to be the arbitrary definition by which one shall know the aspect of a face, an idea, a world, which is valid to 'modernity'? – which will guarantee that a washerwoman shall look like a washerwoman and nothing else as long as she lives? Is there not a dangerous whiff of the esplanade and the bath-chair in this funny arbitration?

One has to ask oneself also, what might the distinguishing features of a washerwoman be? Is she to be a convention or a person? Must she be scrawny and sud-bespattered and over forty-five or fifty-five or sixty-five? Or not? May she never transcend the washtub, her face be never anything but steamily puffy and pink? Or may it?

To me it doesn't seem fair!

According to our Berlin critic, however, it would appear that the virtue of film is the vice of photography. Helmar Lerski has done wrong and seriously wrong in finding distinction – and something else perhaps not instantly definable – in the face of a washerwoman. 'Aristocratic' – that word! The woman I think he means carries a fine enough and dauntless head. But why 'aristocratic' – which seems to have been used with a class connotation, which is *altmodisch* if you will?

Köpfe des Alltags (Heads of Everyday) is a book that appealed to me strongly. I like its gradual sonorous deepening, or piling up, which you will. Turning the pages is to enter a world of dreamy speculation, of *weltgeist,* of strange intimacy. Here is sorrow grown finally laconic. Not the less imminent because of its submission. A kind of fen-land, bleak, massive and mysterious.

There is something that arrests in the so examinable detail of these heads, something almost telescopic, nearness that seems to be about to topple on you. They tell their own tale, there is stress without bias; Helmar Lerski has not 'just run around with a Kodak', but has made observation sensitive and illuminated, leaving finally, through the wilful drama of lighting and tonal quality, the faces to find, like water, their own level of expression.

. . . A mouth that out-thrusts generosity and lust in contrast to the indrawn ambush of eyes habitually wary; eyes as wish-wells: eyes recording past, so they have become mute and rather meaningless like memorials. Here is a face stark-stripped by meanness to essential diagrammatic rudiments: conscious impotence, the down-drawn, tight-edged mouth determination to belittle and envy as goads to self defeat. Follows the mournful idealist, bespectacled, 'an intellectual',– he too has gazed at life with pity and a dream of helping. His corduroy communist's coat is the badge of his yearning to dismiss oppression, to advance his mental programme to the actual.

'Finding their own level of expression', these faces have often noble and sublimated qualities. The effect is far-reaching and entire.

The photographic quality is magnificent. The answer, if any be needed, to painted portraiture – a horrid pastime and anachronistic now as a tandem bicycle.

What is established is clear definition of the physionomical-psychological accord; a blending of visible and 'invisible', so that rather more than character delineation is there. In the 'planetary' – the telescopic – quality I have mentioned lies perhaps a rather significant truth. That these faces more than normally abstract, intimate and unconcerned, as far as scrutiny carries effect, are like the faces we studied as children, when faces were stranger, more to be wondered at, stared at, explored, than at any other time in life. Perhaps part of the secret of this intimacy – part of the mystery and power is sealed in this fact. We have access to these personalities as only children have, and knowledge or experience trailing in wake, strikes odd echoes, so that there is a swinging between present and past. The 'unremembered' is like an electric sky-sign which occasionnally flashes across the conscious, leaving a sense of expectation, wonder and unrest.

Added to which is inevitable appreciation of the slow unfolding, the exploration, the documentation and swift discovery – here is cinema at its best. There is, for once, enough of life and of movement in the inferences here exposed.

The portraits are not enlargements, so they are without the blur and gentleness enlargements are apt to give. Pores of the skin, cracked lips, hairs in the nostrils – these are part of the purpose and reality.

Walter Benjamin 1931

Extract from *A Short History of Photography*

Indeed, Atget's Paris photos are the forerunners of surrealist photography; an advance party of the only really broad column surrealism managed to set in motion. He was the first to disinfect the stifling atmosphere generated by conventional portrait photography in the age of decline. He cleanses this atmosphere, indeed he dispels it altogether: he initiates the emancipation of object from aura which is the most signal achievement of the latest school of photography. When avant-garde periodicals like *Bifur* or *Variété* publish pictures captioned *Westminster, Lille, Antwerp* or *Breslau* but showing only details, here a piece of balustrade, there a tree top whose bar branches criss-cross a gas lamp, or a gable wall, or a lamp-post with a life-buoy bearing the name of the town – this is nothing but a literary refinement of themes that Atget discovered. He looked for what was unremarked, forgotten, cast adrift, and thus such pictures too work against the exotic, romantically sonorous names of the cities; they pump the aura out of reality like water from a sinking ship. What is aura, actually? A strange weave of space and time: the unique appearance or semblance of distance, no matter how close the object may be. While resting on a summer's noon, to trace a range of mountains on the horizon, or a branch that throws its shadow on the observer, until the moment or the hour became part of their appearance – that is what it means to breathe the aura of those mountains, that branch. Now, to bring things *closer* to us, or rather to the masses, is just as passionate an inclination in our day as the overcoming of whatever is unique in every situation by means of its reproduction. Every day the need to possess the object in close-up in the form of a picture, or rather a copy, becomes more imperative. And the difference between the copy, which illustrated papers and newsreels keep in readiness, and the picture is unmistakable. Uniqueness and duration are as intimately conjoined in the latter as are transience and reproducibility in the former. The stripping bare of the object, the destruction of the aura, is the mark of a perception whose sense of the sameness of things has grown to the point where even the singular, the unique, is divested of its uniqueness – by means of its reproduction. Atget almost always passed by the 'great sights and the so-called landmarks'; what he did not pass by was a long row of boot lasts; or the Paris courtyards, where from night to morning the handcarts stand in serried ranks; or the tables after people have finished eating and left, the dishes not yet cleared away as they exist in the hundreds of thousands at the same hour; or the brothel at Rue . . . No 5, whose street number appears, gigantic, at four different places on the building's façade. Remarkably, however, almost all these pictures are empty. Empty the Porte d'Arceuil by the Fortifications, empty the triumphal steps, empty the courtyards, empty, as it should be, the Place du Tertre. They are not lonely, merely without mood; the city in these pictures looks cleared out, like a lodging that has not yet found a new tenant. It is in these achievements that surrealist photography sets the scene for a salutory estrangement between man and his surroundings. It gives free play to the politically educated eye, under whose gaze all intimacies are sacrificed to the illumination of detail.

It is obvious that this new way of seeing stands to gain least in an area where there was the greatest self-indulgence: commercial portrait photography. On

August Sander *Peasant couple (Westerwald)* 1932

the other hand, to do without people is for photography the most impossible of renunciations. And anyone who did not know it was taught by the best of the Russian films that milieu and landscape, too, reveal themselves most readily to those photographers who succeed in capturing their anonymous physiognomy, as it were presenting them at face value. Whether this is possible, however, depends very much on the subject. The generation that was not obsessed with going down to posterity in photographs, rather shyly drawing back into their private space in the face of such proceedings – the way Schopenhauer withdrew into the depths of his chair in the Frankfurt picture, taken about 1850 – for that very reason allowed that space, the space where they lived, to get onto the plate with them. That generation did not pass on its virtues. So the Russian feature film was the first opportunity in decades to put people before the camera who had no use for their photographs. And immediately the human face appeared on film with new and immeasurable significance. But it was no longer a portrait. What was it? It is the outstanding service of a German photographer to have answered this question. August Sander[1] has compiled a series of faces that is in no way inferior to the tremendous physiognomic gallery mounted by an Eisenstein or a Pudovkin, and he has done it from a scientific viewpoint. 'His complete work comprises seven groups which correspond to the existing social order, and is to be published in some 45 folios containing 12 photographs each.' So far we have a sample volume containing 60 reproductions, which offer inexhaustible material for study. 'Sander starts off with the peasant, the earth-bound man, takes the observer through every social stratum and every walk of life up to the highest representatives of civilization, and then back down all the way to the idiot.' The author did not approach this enormous undertaking as a scholar, or with the advice of ethnographers and sociologists, but, as the publisher says, 'from direct observation'. It was assuredly a very impartial, indeed bold sort of observation, but delicate too, very much in the spirit of Goethe's remark: 'There is a delicate empiricism which so intimately involves itself with the object that it becomes true theory'. So it was quite in order for an observer like Döblin to have hit on precisely the scientific aspects of this work, commenting: 'Just as there is comparative anatomy, which helps us to understand the nature and history of organs, so this photographer is doing comparative photography, adopting a scientific standpoint superior to the photographer of detail'. It would be a pity if economic considerations should prevent the continuing publication of this extraordinary body of work. Apart from this basic encouragement, there is a more specific incentive one might offer the publisher. Work like Sander's could overnight assume unlooked-for topicality. Sudden shifts of power such as are now overdue in our society can make the ability to read facial types a matter of vital importance. Whether one is of the left or right, one will have to get used to being looked at in terms of one's provenance. And one will have to look at others the same way. Sander's work is more than a picture book. It is a training manual.

'In our age there is no work of art that is looked at so closely as a photograph of oneself, one's closest relatives and friends, one's sweetheart', wrote Lichtwark back in 1907, thereby moving the enquiry out of the realm of aesthetic distinctions into that of social functions. Only from this vantage point can it be carried further. It is indeed significant that the debate has raged most fiercely around the aesthetics of *photography as art,* whereas the far less questionable social fact of *art as photography* was given scarcely a glance. And yet the impact of the photographic reproduction of art works is of very much greater importance for the function of art than the greater or lesser artistry of a photography that regards all experience as fair game for the camera. The amateur who returns home with great piles of artistic shots is in fact no more appealing a figure than the hunter who comes back with quantities of game of no use to anyone but the dealer. And the day does indeed seem to be at hand when there will be more illustrated magazines than game merchants. So much for the *snapshot.* But the emphasis changes completely if we turn from photography-as-art to art-as-photography. Everyone will have noticed how much easier it is to get hold of a picture, more particularly a piece of sculpture, not to mention architecture, in a photograph than in reality. It is all too tempting to blame this squarely on the

1. August Sander, *Das Antlitz der Zeit,* Berlin, 1930

decline of artistic appreciation, on a failure of contemporary sensibility. But one is brought up short by the way the understanding of great works was transformed at about the same time the techniques of reproduction were being developed. They can no longer be regarded as the work of individuals; they have become a collective creation, a corpus so vast it can be assimilated only through miniaturization. In the final analysis, mechanical reproduction is a technique of diminution that helps men to achieve a control over works of art without whose aid they could no longer be used.

If one thing typifies present-day relations between art and photography, it is the unresolved tension between the two introduced by the photography of works of art. Many of those who, as photographers, determine the present face of this technology started out as painters. They turned their back on painting after attempts to bring its expressive resources into a living and unequivocal relationship with modern life. The keener their feel for the temper of the times, the more problematic their starting point became for them. For once again, as 80 years before, photography was taking over from painting. 'The creative potential of the new', says Moholy-Nagy, 'is for the most part slowly revealed through old forms, old instruments and areas of design that in their essence have already been superseded by the new, but which under pressure from the new as it takes shape are driven to a euphoric efflorescence. Thus, for example, futurist (structural) painting brought forth the clearly defined *Problematik* of the simultaneity of motion, the representation of the instant, which was later to destroy it – and this at a time when film was already known but far from being understood . . . Similarly, some of the painters (neoclassicists and verists) today using representational-objective methods can be regarded – with caution – as forerunners of a new representational optical form which will soon be making use only of mechanical, technical methods.' And Tristan Tzara, 1922: 'When everything that called itself art was stricken with palsy, the photographer switched on his thousand candle-power lamp and gradually the light-sensitive paper absorbed the darkness of a few everyday objects. He had discovered what could be done by a pure and sensitive flash of light that was more important than all the constellations arranged for the eye's pleasure'. The photographers who went over from figurative art to photography not on opportunistic grounds, not by chance, not out of sheer laziness, today constitute the avant-garde among their colleagues, because they are to some extent protected by their background against the greatest danger facing photography today, the touch of the commercial artist. 'Photography as art', says Sasha Stone, 'is a very dangerous thing.'

Where photography takes itself out of context, severing the connections illustrated by Sander, Blossfeld or Germaine Krull, where it frees itself from physiognomic, political and scientific interest, then it becomes *creative*. The lens now looks for interesting juxtapositions; photography turns into a sort of arty journalism. 'The spirit that overcomes mechanics translates exact findings into parables of life.' The more far-reaching the crisis of the present social order, the more rigidly its individual components are locked together in their death struggle, the more has the creative – in its deepest essence a sport, by contradiction out of imitation – become a fetish, whose lineaments live only in the fitful illumination of changing fashion. The creative in photography is its capitulation to fashion. *The world is beautiful* – that is its watchword. Therein is unmasked the posture of a photography that can endow any soup can with cosmic significance but cannot grasp a single one of the human connexions in which it exists, even where most far-fetched subjects are more concerned with saleability than with insight. But because the true face of this kind of photographic creativity is the advertisement or association, its logical counterpart is the act of unmasking or construction. As Brecht says, 'The situation is complicated by the fact that

Albert Renger-Patzsch *Pulley wheel, Siemens Elektrowärme G.m.b.H. Neu-Sörnewitz*

less than ever does the mere reflexion of reality reveal anything about reality. A photograph of the Krupp works or the A.E.G. tells us next to nothing about these institutions. Actual reality has slipped into the functional. The reification of human relations – the factory, say – means that they are no longer explicit. So something must in fact be *built up*, something artificial, posed.' We owe it to the surrealists that they trained the pioneers of such a constructivist photography. A further stage in this contest between creative and constructivist photography is typified by the Russian film. It is not too much to say that the great achievements of the Russian directors were only possible in a country where photography does not set out to charm or persuade, but to experiment and instruct. In this sense, and in this only, there is still some meaning in the grandiloquent salute offered to photography in 1855 by the uncouth painter of ideas, Antoine Wiertz. 'For some years now the glory of our age has been a machine which daily amazes the mind and startles the eye. Before another century is out, this machine will be the brush, the palette, the colours, the craft, the experience, the patience, the dexterity, the sureness of touch, the atmosphere, the lustre, the exemplar, the perfection, the very essence of painting . . . Let no one suppose that daguerrotype photography will be the death of art . . . When the daguerrotype, that infant prodigy, has grown to its full stature, when all its art and its strength have been revealed, then will Genius seize it by the scruff of the neck and shout: Come with me, you are mine now! We shall work together!' How sober, indeed pessimistic by contrast are the words in which Baudelaire announced the new technology to his readers, two years later, in the *Salon of 1857*. Like the preceding quotations, they can be read today only with a subtle shift of emphasis. But as a counterpart to the above, they still make sense as a violent reaction to the encroachments of artistic photography. 'In these sorry days a new industry has arisen that has done not a little to strengthen the asinine belief . . . that art is and can be nothing other than the accurate reflection of nature . . . A

John Heartfield *The Atmosphere in Geneva*
Front cover of *Arbeiter-Illustrierte-Zeitung* 1932

vengeful god has hearkened to the voice of this multitude. Daguerre is his Messiah.' And: 'If photography is permitted to supplement some of art's functions, they will forthwith be usurped and corrupted by it, thanks to photography's natural alliance with the mob. It must therefore revert to its proper duty, which is to serve as the handmaiden of science and the arts.'

One thing, however, both Wiertz and Baudelaire failed to grasp: the lessons inherent in the authenticity of the photograph. These cannot be forever circumvented by a commentary whose clichés merely establish verbal associations in the viewer. The camera is getting smaller and smaller, ever readier to capture fleeting and secret moments whose images paralyse the associative mechanisms in the beholder. This is where the caption comes in, whereby photography turns all life's relationships into literature, and without which all constructivist photography must remain arrested in the approximate. Not for nothing have Atget's photographs been likened to those of the scene of a crime. But is not every square inch of our cities the scene of a crime? Every passer-by a culprit? Is it not the task of the photographer – descendant of the augurs and haruspices – to reveal guilt and to point out the guilty in his pictures? 'The illiteracy of the future', someone has said, 'will be ignorance not of reading or writing, but of photography.' But must not a photographer who cannot read his own pictures be no less accounted an illiterate? Will not the caption become the most important part of the photograph? Such are the questions in which the interval of 90 years that separates us from the age of the daguerrotype discharge its historical tension. It is in the illumination of these sparks that the first photographs emerge, beautiful and unapproachable, from the darkness of our grandfathers' day.

Hannah Höch *Good Company* 1925

Beaumont Newhall 1977

Photo Eye of the 1920's
The Deutsche Werkbund Exhibition of 1929

In the throbbing avant-garde art world of the 1920s, played a major role. No longer did artists and critics look down upon the camera; they embraced it with enthusiasm. As we look over the art literature of the period, particularly German publications, we find a surprising interest in photography, even among art historians, who previously had paid little heed to its significance. For example, Hans Hildebrand, in his 1924 *Kunst des 19. and 20. Jahrhunderts*[1] describes Daguerre's invention, and the later section of the book reproduces a photogram by Man Ray and a photomontage by Paul Citroen, both made only a few years before the book was published. Heinrich Schwarz, in his *David Octavius Hill, Meister der Photographie,*[2] a collection of calotypes taken by Hill and Robert Adamson in Edinburgh in the 1840s, expresses the need for art historians to take photography into account as a major force in the stylistic determination of modern painting at the turn of the century. Many of the art periodicals of the 1920s, such as *Die Form, Das Kunstblatt, Die Kunstchronik, Cahiers d'art,* had frequent reproductions of photographs and critical articles on photographers and their work.

By the end of the decade photography had become of sufficient importance for the Deutsche Werkbund to organize a large and imposing international exhibition, 'Film und Foto', in the municipal exposition building of Stuttgart from May 18 to July 7, 1929.

The Deutsche Werkbund was a prestigious organization. Founded in 1907, it was an outgrowth of the arts and crafts movement of the turn of the century stemming from William Morris. But whereas Morris sought for the revival of hand craft in the age of the machine, the Deutsche Werkbund sought for the reconciliation of art and technology. It was through the Deutsche Werkbund that Walter Gropius got his start as a great modern architect and founder of the Bauhaus. In 1927 the Deutsche Werkbund put on an extraordinary exhibition of modern architecture. They convinced the city fathers of Stuttgart to commission the most advanced modern architects to build a complete, working housing development, the Wiessenhofsiedlung. The buildings were designed by Gropius, Mies Van Der Rohe, O. J. P. Oud, and Le Corbusier; after 50 years they still stand, a monument to the 'International Style'.

With the same seriousness of purpose, the Deutsche Werkbund two years later approached the problem of photography. Our documentation of the 'Film und Foto' exhibition is scanty. Happily a catalogue was published;[3] its 21 illustrations can be supplemented by the 76 reproductions in *Foto Auge/Oeil et Photo/Photo Eye,* edited by Franz Roh and Jan Tschichold.[4] Of the 40 photographers whose work is reproduced in this book, only three do not appear in the Stuttgart exhibition catalogue.

The list of those responsible for the exhibition is an indication of the serious way in which photography was considered. The director was Gustaf Stotz of the

1. Hans Hildebrand, *Kunst des 19. und 20. Jahrhunderts,* Berlin, 1924.
2. Heinrich Schwarz, *David Octavius Hill, Meister der Photographie,* Leipzig, 1931.
3. *International Ausstellung des Deutschen Werkbunds Film und Foto,* Stuttgart, 1929.
4. Franz Roh and Jan Tschichold, eds., *Foto-Auge/Oeil et Photo/Photo Eye; 76 Photos of the Period,* Stuttgart, 1929. Facsimile reprints were published in 1973 by The Arno Press, New York and the Verlag Ernst Wasmuth, Tübingen. The illustrations of the latter are far superior to the former.

Württenburg section – Arbeitsgemeinschaft – of the Werkbund. There was an executive committee of three: Hans Hildebrandt, professor of art history in Stuttgart; Bernhard Pankok, architect of the exposition hall and professor at the Gewerbeschule in Stuttgart; and Jan Tschichold, the typographer who revolutionized printing in Germany by introducing the use of simple type faces, asymmetrical layout and photographs integrated with words, particularly in advertising. Listed as collaborators were those who helped choose the photographs; of these the most notable were: Laszlo Moholy-Nagy, formerly a master at the Bauhaus but at the time freelancing as a designer in Berlin; Edward Weston, who not only chose work by West Coast photographers in America, but contributed a statement for the catalogue; Edward Steichen of New York; Piet Zwart of Amsterdam; El Lissitzsky of the Soviet Union, in association with the Organization for Cultural Relations Between the USSR and Other Countries; the Secretary General of the Schweizer Werkbund, Zurich; and Sigfried Giedion, art historian, theorizer and proselytizer of modern architecture, Zurich. Only three of the collaborators were practising photographers: Steichen, Weston, and Moholy-Nagy.

'Fifo' – as the exhibition came to be called – was announced in the fall of 1928:

This exhibition will bring together for the first time work of those people, at home and abroad, who have broken new paths in photography as well as film. Besides the work of the film *avant-garde* to which belong Eggling, Hans Richter, Léger, Cavalcanti, the Russians and others, there will be work of the pioneers in the field of photography and phototypography,[5] like Man Ray, Paris, Steichen and Sheeler, New York, Lissitzky, Moscow, Piet Zwart, Amsterdam, as well as Moholy-Nagy, Heartfield, Schwitters, Tschichold and others in Germany. In addition are extraordinary productions of anonymous news photographers from all over the world and photographs from various areas of technology and science.[6]

The director gave further details of the exhibition in the May issue of *Das Kunstblatt*. He stated that the purpose of the show was to demonstrate the new means of creating form given us by lens, camera, and highly sensitive film:

A new optic has developed. We see things differently now, without painterly intent in the impressionistic sense. Today things are important that earlier were hardly noticed: for example shoe lasts, gutters, spools of thread, fabrics, machines, etc. They interest us for their material substance, for the simple quality of the thing-in-itself; they interest as the means of creating space-form on surfaces, as the bearers of the darkness and the light – (The darkess and the light – basic form-creation of photography!).

And the fixing of time. Highly sensitive plates, lenses of great light-gathering power, permit us to snatch the most swift motion. (Photographs of a flying bullet!) That means that photography can go beyond the representation of the inanimate, the still life; it can seize life in action, even violent action. Photographs of this kind are 'contemporary'.

The results that can be obtained uniquely by these new photographic means have been published here and there but never systematically compiled. The Stuttgart exhibition will attempt to do this. The fields that will be investigated are extensive. To name a few: news photography in the widest sense, including sport shots, war pictures, street pictures, night exposures, criminological photographs. Further: scientific photographs – zoological, botanical, medical (X-rays) – photomicrographs, aerial views, studies of the structure of materials. Then the area of light made form-giving by artifical sources, some with the lens, others directly on light-sensitive paper (photograms); the superposition of several photographs; the use of photography in the graphic arts and advertising (photomontage and phototypography).[7]

There were 14 galleries in the exposition building. The exact number of

5. Phototypography: a word coined to cover the whole field of photomontage and the mixture of type and the photographic image, particularly as used in advertising and poster design; not to be confused with phototypesetting.
6. 'Werkbund-Ausstellung Film und Foto, Stuttgart, 1929,' *Die Form*, IV, February 15, 1929, 95.
7. Gustaf Stotz, 'Werkbund Ausstellung "Film und Foto", Stuttgart, 1929,' *Das Kunstblatt*, V, 1929, 154.

photographs shown is not recorded; the catalogue contains 940 entries. Some are the titles of individual prints, but many refer to groups of unspecified size. To Moholy-Nagy was given the task of installing the theme show – an exhibition-within-an-exhibition – in the first gallery, through which all visitors passed to the remaining 13 galleries. Thus far I have found no record of it, nor installation photographs. But Moholy-Nagy's book, *Painting, Photography, Film* of 1925,[8] is so close in content to Stotz's scenario that we can assume that the theme show was similar.

Moholy-Nagy was a pioneer in the recognition of what I choose to call the *found photograph*. Just as Marcel Duchamp transformed a utilitarian bottle rack into a piece of sculpture by selecting it and isolating it and exhibiting it, so did Moholy-Nagy elevate a news photograph taken by nobody-knows-whom to aesthetic consideration by creating for it a new context in an exhibition, or within the covers of a book. In 1922, while still a member of the MA ('Today') group of Hungarian artists he produced, with Ludwig Kasak, a *Book of New Artists*,[9] explaining the new 'isms'. Vanguard works of art were juxtaposed to photographs of machines. There were no captions, and thus the book was a non-verbal, totally innovative form of explanation. In *Painting, Photography, Film* Moholy-Nagy again relied upon juxtaposition – or can we not call it, in the Eisenstein sense, montage? Opposite a photograph of cranes in flight he placed a formation of five airplanes. He paired a dancer at mid-leap with a motorcycle rider: caption, *Racing Tempo Immobilized*. He teased the reader: on the left page, a highly constructivist picture of airplanes in flight seen through the wings and struts of the camera-carrying airplane; on the right an up-shot of what the caption identifies as the largest clock in the world but unrecognizable as such. His comment: 'The experience of the oblique view, and displaced proportions.'

In another spread he put a photograph by Albert Renger-Patzsch of a factory chimney seen looking upwards from its base opposite a puzzle picture: the church of St Paul's in London as seen from the top of the dome looking straight down on the pews beneath.

This is very typical of the kind of vision that Moholy-Nagy and his contemporaries of the 1920s enjoyed so much. They not only found photographs, but they found photographs in their own photographs, as I learned one day when Moholy-Nagy was showing me some of his prints. He had a pile of them on his desk and after we had looked at one, he would throw it on the floor. Suddenly, after showing me a dockside photograph, he stood up and said in excitement, 'Isn't that coil of rope there beautiful? I never saw it before.'

Moholy-Nagy also included an example of what he called 'virtual sculpture': a time exposure made at night in Bremen in which the headlights of trolley cars and automobiles form light tracks and, of course, aerial photographs which were just then becoming appreciated for their beauty, not only by those interested in photography, but in general. When Ernest Hemingway was filing copy to the *Toronto Star* from Europe, he described his first flight in an airplane in 1922:

We headed almost straight east of Paris . . . and the ground began to flatten out beneath us. It looked cut into brown squares, yellow squares, green squares and big flat blotches of green where there was a forest. I began to understand cubist painting.[10]

El Lissitzsky, the Russian constructivist, collected aerial photographs, and his fellow countryman Kasimir Malevich defined the Suprematist environment by a

8. Laszlo Moholy-Nagy, *Malerei, Photographie, Film*, Bauhausbuch 8, München, 1925. A revised edition was published in 1927; it has been reprinted in facsimile by Florian Kupferberg, Mainz and Berlin, 1967. An English translation, *Painting, Photography, Film*, was published by Lund Humphries, London, and by the MIT Press, Cambridge, Massachusetts, 1969, with repagination.

9. Ludwig Kassak and Laszlo Moholy-Nagy, eds., *Buch neuer Künstler*, Wien, 1922.

10. Ernest Hemingway, 'A Paris to Strasbourg Flight,' *Toronto Daily Star*, September 9, 1922, in *By-Line Ernest Hemingway*, New York, 1968, 38.

page of air views in his *The Non-Objective World*,[11] published in the Bauhaus Book series in 1927.

The photomicrograph reveals what the eye unaided cannot see – the feet of a barnacle, or the strange crablike body of a louse, menacing in its giant size, beautiful in its sculptural form and graphic in its articulation.

Astronomical photography, in which the telescope is a space camera based on planet Earth, follows neither the rules of naturalistic perspective nor stylistic conventions. With special prismatic lenses the light of the stars can be spread in bands from which scientists can discover the elements of each star shown. The ever beautiful spiral nebulae display the basic forms reduced from their immensity to a graphic symbol.

The X-ray often reveals more than bone structure. Thus a radiograph of a frog shows the skeleton with a mysterious aura of seemingly textureless flesh surrounding it. On the other hand the so-called 'soft' X-rays that penetrate only a short distance beneath the surface reveal the total structure.

The negative as an end, rather than a means, fascinated Moholy-Nagy. The Stuttgart exhibition showed several; one of the most striking was looking down upon a tugboat on the Elbe river by Andreas Feininger, son of the painter and later to be a staff photographer for *Life* magazine. Moholy-Nagy published one of his own negatives as a print: it shows a woman standing; her head is bent so the hair becomes the very centre of the composition, a white form, seemingly detached from the body. Beneath it he wrote: 'The transposition of the tone-values transposes the relationships too. The small amount of white becomes most strikingly visible and so determines the character of the whole picture.'[12] He found it extraordinary that the very parts of the scene where there was little or no light visible themselves become light in the negative.

It is curious that W. F. Fox Talbot, inventor of the negative–positive process, should have appreciated the negative for these qualities. In 1839 he wrote:

The effect of the copy though of course unlike the original (substituting as it does light for shadow and vice versa) yet is often singularly pleasing and would I think often suggest to artists useful ideas respecting light and shade.[13]

In this first gallery of 'Fifo' there was also an historical section, from the collection of Erich Stenger.[14] What was shown, unfortunately, was neither recorded in the catalogue, nor commented upon in the press; but the inclusion of the history of photography by the organizers of the exhibition is significant, for it may well be the earliest recognition of the field by an art-oriented organization.

Due to lack of documentation, I can only sketch what was shown in the other galleries of the exhibition. The reviews especially praised the American contributions. It appears that Weston was chosen as a collaborator because of his friendship with the modern architect Richard Neutra, who brought the 'International Style' to Los Angeles when he moved there in 1926. Weston had dinner with him on January 3, 1929, and wrote about the meeting in his daybook: 'Representing in America an important exhibit of photography to be held in Germany this summer, he has given me complete charge of collecting the exhibit, choosing the ones whose work I consider worthy of showing, and of writing the catalogue foreword to the American group.'[15]

The foreword is a concise statement of his functional approach to photogra-

11. Kasimir Malevich, *The Non-Objective World*, Chicago, 1959. A translation of *Die gegenstandsclose Welt*, Bauhausbuch 12, 1927.

12. Moholy-Nagy, *Painting, Photography, Film*, 1969, 98.

13. Quoted without source by D. B. Thomas in the catalogue of the Arts Council of Great Britain exhibition 'From Today Painting is Dead'; *The beginnings of Photography*, London, Victoria and Albert Museum, 1972, 30.

14. The Stenger collection is now owned by Agfa-Gevaert, manufacturers of photographic materials, and is on public display in their 'Foto Historama' in Leverkusen, Germany. See the description by Helmut Gernsheim, *Foto Historama Agfa-Gevaert*, Leverkusen, n.d., 5–14.

15. Edward Weston, *The Daybooks; II, California*, Nancy Newhall, ed., Millerton, New York, n.d. (c.1973), 103.

phy. Of the 20 of his own photographs that Weston chose, the *Sharpshooter*, as it was titled, was reproduced in the catalogue. It is a portrait of his friend, the Mexican senator Manuel Hernandez Galván, taken in 1924 with a handheld reflex camera at the instant when the senator pulled the trigger of his revolver at target practice. That Weston was able to release his shutter at the same instant pleased him; getting the fleeting facial expression of his sitter instantaneously was a far cry from making the posed studio portraits he relied upon for his living. To the art historian Carl Georg Heise this photography was 'one of the peak productions of the whole exhibition'.[16]

Whether the photograph catalogued simply as 'jugs' is the *Tres Ollas de Oaxaca* of 1926 we can only surmise: a simple photograph of three black clay pots, it is one of Edward Weston's finest works of the Mexican period, of utter simplicity in directness and form. René d'Harnoncourt, who later became Director of the Museum of Modern Art in New York, exclaimed, when Weston showed him the photograph in Mexico, 'This print is the beginning of a new art.'[17] One of Weston's nudes was shown, quite possibly the highly abstract torso of Anita Brenner, with back to camera – a strong, deep personification, so to speak, of Weston's drive to the isolation of form without loss of substance. He also sent studies of shells, seen in a similar fashion, filling the negative with their glistening, almost incandescent forms. Less well known are Weston's still life arrangments of *juguetes* – little toys sold at peasant markets. One was chosen for reproduction by the periodical *Photographische Rundschau*, a female doll against a broad-brimmed hat – reminiscent, in its asymmetrical placement of elements and flatness of field, of his earliest work, but with the addition of textural substance.

Edward Weston chose twenty pictures made by his son Brett, who began photographing in Mexico with his father's Graflex camera when he was not yet fourteen. His *Tin Roofs* of 1925 already shows his concern with form and substance. The shape of the shadowed area, its utter blackness, dominates the picture. It was reproduced in Roh and Tschichold's *Photo-Eye*. A few years ago, Brett tried to reconstruct for me his Stuttgart group from the listed titles: he believed that the photograph of lily stalks, which he remembered as his first photograph, was one of them, and also a geometrical study of circles within circles in an end-on view of a pile of sewer pipes. *Rocks* may well have been one of the earliest photographs he made in 1929 at Point Lobos, California.

Imogen Cunningham was represented largely by her plant forms, views of flowers and plants taken in close-up, but not enlarged beyond recognition. To judge from the number that were reproduced in the popular photographic press, they were much appreciated. Exactly fitting the style so favoured in Germany in the 1920s was the *Shredded Wheat Tower*, a view looking straight up at the bottom of a water tank, with the girders supporting it appearing radially.

We have no exact knowledge of the photographs by Edward Steichen that were shown. He was, at this time, working in a distinctly different manner than the soft focus negatives, the gum-bichromate prints, the picturesque subject matter and the Whistler-inspired style that had brought him European fame when they were first exhibited in London in 1900 and in Paris in 1901. He, too, photographed flower forms – with the exactness of the horticulturist which had become his avocation in the post-World War I years. We know that six of his fashion photographs were lent to the show by the German editor of *Vogue*. Steichen was then working for its publisher, Condé Nast, and had introduced a highly theatrical style well shown in *The Dramatic Silhouette* featured in the

16. Carl Georg Heise, *"Film und Foto,"* zur Ausstellung der Deutschen Werkbundes in Stuttgart,' *Lübecker Generalsanzeiger*, June 18, 1929.
17. Edward Weston, *The Daybooks;* I, Mexico, Nancy Newhall, ed., Millerton, New York, n.d. (*c.*1973), 188.

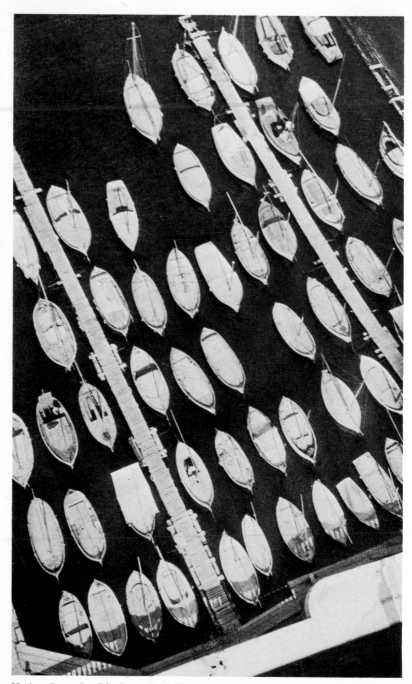

Herbert Bayer *Small harbour, Marseilles* 1928

April 27 issue of the American edition of *Vogue*. Steichen also produced photographs of celebrities for the Condé Nast publication, *Vanity Fair*, of which the photograph of Greta Garbo is typical, making of her face the mask that marked her theatrical fame.

Charles Sheeler, Steichen's friend and, at this time, his collaborator at Condé Nast, sent ten photographs, unspecified in the catalogue. That his *White Barn* of 1915 was included I know from a letter he wrote me in answer to my request to reproduce that now-famous early work.

Dear Beaumont: As for the White Barn you referred to in your letter it has been retired on pension, it having been in circulation since about 1915. Most recently in the M.M.A. [Museum of Modern Art] catalogue celebrating the 25 Anniversary and going back to Broom in the early 20s, in the Photo and Film show Stuttgart 1929 and so far into the night. If there is anything else you would care to have let me know . . .[18]

Sheeler's New York City photographs had already interested Europe: a portfolio of them appeared in the French *avant-garde* magazine *Cahiers d'Art* in 1927,[14] and some of these, as well as his Ford Plant series, were quite possibly shown at Stuttgart. Sheeler visited the exhibition; on the same European trip he made the memorable series of photographs of Chartres Cathedral.

Two other Americans especially interested the Germans: Ralph Steiner and Paul Outerbridge, Jr. A layout of their work, with the following caption, appeared in *Das Kunstblatt* for 1926:

Photography in America
Precision work. Exact representation of form. No pictorial romanticism. Unconditional involvement with technique. Pushing technical possibilities to the utmost. Clear picture architecture. Emphasis on plastic values. Concerned interest in the form world of everyday surroundings. Through close-ups things take on a new aspect.[20]

In the same spirit as these American photographers is the work of the German Albert Renger-Patzsch, whose book *Die Welt ist Schon* (The World is Beautiful),[21] appeared in 1928. The word 'Welt' in the title should be emphasized, for the message of the book to abstract painters in their studios was: 'Get outside and look at the world.' The introduction was by Carl Georg Heise, the art historian whose praise of Edward Weston we have noted. The book is organized by subject: plant forms, such as the thorny cactus that Moholy-Nagy chose for his *Painting, Photography, Film*, animals, as in a close-up of the eye of a coiled snake, and especially the strident forms of industrial constructions (blast furnaces, cranes, and heavy machinery).

Hugo Erfurth, of Dresden, a photographer surprisingly overlooked today, showed massive portraits at Stuttgart. He had begun as Steichen had begun, in the pictorial period, with soft focus and emphasis on the silhouette, but changed to a sharp, clear and direct style. His portrait of Käthe Kollwitz is as hard and as relentless as her lithographs; she looks unflinchingly straight at the camera with that sense of sympathy so associated with her own portraits of people. It is not surprising that Erfurth was a friend of Otto Dix, who was a prominent member of the group called *Die Neue Sachlichkeit,* the New Objectivity, concerned with fact, with the detailed outward appearance of the world – its thingness, to more literally translate the German.

Apart from the historical section that we have noted, only one photographer not living in 1929 was shown. That was Eugène Atget, who had died in Paris just two years earlier, recognized only by a few photographers. His pictures of Paris appealed to the Surrealists and their choice is echoed in the reproduction in the

18. Charles Sheeler, letter to Beaumont Newhall, undated.
19. Portfolio of photographs of New York by Charles Sheeler, *Cahiers d'Art*, No. 4–5, 1927, 180–2.
20. 'Photographie in America,' *Das Kunstblatt*, X, 1926, 447.
21. Albert Renger-Patzsch, *Die Welt is Schön*, München, 1928.

catalogue, a shop on the rue du petit Domal in Paris; a corset shop on the Boulevard de Strasbourg was also chosen for reproduction by the periodical *Photographische Rundschau.*

In contrast to the 'straight photographs' we have mentioned was the quantity of 'experimental' work on display, photographs obviously within the style of the abstract and Surreal painters of the period. Moholy-Nagy and Man Ray stand out. Moholy-Nagy had a passion for pointing the camera up and the camera down to reveal usually-unseen forms. Of his photograph *Spring, 1928* – a view from his Berlin apartment looking down on a man in a treetop, pruning – he wrote: 'A bird's eye view of trees which form a unity with the pattern of the street. The lines running in many directions, placed each behind the other, form a very rich spatial network.'[22] His *From a Radio Tower, Berlin, 1928* is in effect an aerial photograph. Or he pointed his camera up, as in the *Bauhaus Balconies,* revelling in the convergence of verticals considered distortion by most text books. A still life, *Mirrors and Reflections,* was reproduced by *The Little Review* in 1926.[23] Edward Weston saw it and was puzzled: 'it only brings a question – why?' he wrote in his daybook.[24] Yet the photograph points the way to Moholy-Nagy's *Light-Space Modulator,* completed in 1930, the pioneer kinetic sculpture on which he based his film, *Light Play: Black, White, Gray.*

A favourite subject for Moholy-Nagy and his Bauhaus colleague, the designer and typographer Herbert Bayer, were views from the transporter Bridge in Marseilles, looking down on the quayside and passing fishing craft, seen through the girders of the structure. Some of these photographs are extreme in their bold design and the reliance on brilliant, dazzling light. I remember spending a weekend with Sibyl and Laszlo Moholy-Nagy at their summer house in Chicago in 1946. It was a cloudy day. I was wandering around the farm with my camera when Moholy said, 'Why, Beaumont, you can't photograph today. There's no sunlight.' I thought this a naïveté until I reflected for a minute, and then I realized that all of his photographs have very deep shadows and brilliant highlights.

The same is true of those pictures made without a camera that he called 'photograms'. Objects – opaque and translucent – are placed on light sensitive paper and exposed to light from various sources. The result is a negative: white beneath the opaque objects, gray beneath the translucent objects, and maximum black where the paper was bare. All of Moholy's photograms that I have seen, with a few exceptions, are negatives.

The same technique was used by the American Dadaist and Surrealist painter Man Ray in 1922 while eking out a livelihood in Paris as a photographer: his portfolio *Champs Délicieux* of 12 Rayographs, as he called them, appeared in December of that year with a foreword by Tristan Tzara, spokesman for the Dada group.[25] Priority for the invention of these cameraless photographs was claimed by both Moholy-Nagy and Man Ray. It now appears that Man Ray was the first, on evidence given in Sophie Lissitzky-Küpper's fine biography of her husband, the Russian constructivist, El Lissitzky.[26] But the question is academic. The technique was well known, ever since W. H. Fox Talbot made public his 'photogenic drawing' process in 1839. A 'how-to-do-it' book was even published for amateurs in 1920: *Photographie ohne Kamera* [Photography without Camera].[27]

22. L. Moholy-Nagy, 'Space-Time and the Photographer,' *The American Annual of Photography — 1943,* Boston, 1942, 14.
23. *The Little Review,* XII, Summer, 1926, between 24–25.
24. Edward Weston, *The Daybooks, Mexico,* 190.
25. Man Ray, *Les Champs Délicieux, Album de photographies, avec un préface de Tristan Tzara,* Paris, 1922.
26. S. Lissitzky-Küppers, *El Lissitzky: Life, Letters, Texts,* Greenwich, Conn., 1968, 67.
27. Paul Linder, *Photographie ohne Camera,* Berlin, 1920.

What is important is the vision: Moholy's photograms are architectonic, even cold; Man Ray's hold a sense of mystery. In the choice and juxtaposition of the chosen objects they approach the anecdotal. He sent 22 of them to the Stuttgart exhibition: a motif based upon a fan laid over a hand and a triangle was reproduced in the catalogue, and one of a hand approaching a spherical shape was reproduced in a periodical. There were many other photograms catalogued, some by Kurt Schwitters.

One of the liveliest sections of the exhibition were photomontages: *Portrait of W. Herzfelde* by George Grosz – perhaps more fittingly described as a collage because of the dominance of paint in the picture, but catalogued as a photomontage – several unspecified works by John Heartfield, and 17 by Hannah Höch, including her powerful *Pretty Girl* and *From Above*.

The critics found these Dada photomontages the weakest part of the exhibition, and dismissed Höch's satires as caricatures. Moholy-Nagy's photomontages – a field in which he excelled – were constructivist, and relied upon a graphic network of lines to hold the elements in place. Of his *Leda and the Swan*, 1925, he wrote:

Linear elements, structural pattern, close-up and isolated figures are here the elements for a space articulation. Pasted on a white surface these elements seem to be embedded in infinite space, with clear articulation of nearness and distance. The best description of their effect would be perhaps to say that each element is pasted on vertical glass panes, which are set up in an endless series each behind the other.[28]

El Lissitzky produced one of the most appreciated photomontages of the entire exhibition, *The Constructor, 1924*. It shows his hand holding a compass double-exposed with his face. It is purely photographic, not pasted up, printed from negatives taken for the purpose plus a photogram. The regard he held for photography as a medium is seen in his inclusion of a big enlargement of one of the negatives of *The Constructor* in the exhibition of his paintings in Dresden, 1926.

Two books are related to the 'Film und Foto' exhibition. *Foto Auge/Oeil et Photo/Photo Eye*, by Franz Roh and Jan Tschichold, 1929,[29] with a trilingual text and 76 plates, is a summary, a record of the exhibition: the reproductions appear to have been made from the photographs on display. The layout presents stimulating juxtapositions:

Left	Right
An immense crowd of people. Photographer: anonymous (Russian)	The speaker. Extreme close-up of a mouth. Photographer: P. E. Hahn
Roofs of corrugated iron. Photographer: Brett Weston	Legs, on sand. Photographer: Herbert Bayer
From above, photomontage by Hannah Höch – heads and bodies looking down on chimney, landscape	'Bathing Beach' a hippopotamus wallowing in water. No credit.

On the very day of the opening of 'Fifo', the magazine *Die Form* announced the publication of *Es kommt der neue Fotograf!* (Here comes the New Photographer) by Werner Gräff,[30] a member of the Deutsche Werkbund. It is an

28. Moholy-Nagy, 'Space-Time and the Photographer,' 14.
29. Roh and Tschichold, *Foto-Auge*.
30. *Werner Gräff, Es kommt der neue Fotograf!* Berlin, 1929.

unusual experiment in book design, for the photographs are placed on the page wherever they are called for by the text, even to the extent of breaking sentences. The New Photographer looks up at buildings, to the sky. He looks down. Photographs from above defy central perspective: a horseman, a woman carrying an opened umbrella, a man walking take on unfamiliar forms. Gräff places a close-up of a bald head beside a lighting fixture – and then pairs two photographs taken with the lens 'close to the feet of a man lying on the grass, or the foot of a man pushing a wheel barrow' – 'too close' in the conventional rulebook to avoid the exaggerated scale of the foreshortened image of the man's boots. But the New Photographer revels in this 'distortion' – 'he moves the lens closer to the body' – giving an effect which the critic James Thrall Soby once maintained was used by the painter Pavel Tchelitchew. Gräff illustrated photomontage, how the New Photographer can multiply, by pasting copies of the same two uniformed men side by side to produce, seemingly, a squad of 16; on the opposite page he reproduced a 'photo drawing' by Willy Baumeister: a fragmented photograph of the legs and torso of a nude diving to which are added line drawing of her head and arms. He concludes with a chapter on cameras for the amateur: he recommended the new, flexible and mobile Leica, which had then been on the market for only four years. He prophesied exactly that the 35mm camera would be the camera of the future

As the title of the exhibition indicates, the Deutsche Werkbund was equally concerned with explaining the capabilities and potentials of motion pictures. This took place in the form of a film festival, organized by Hans Richter, and held in a movie theatre in Stuttgart, the Königsbau-Lichtspiele, from June 13 to 26, 1929. It was, in effect, independent of the photographic show and was reviewed by the press separately – a division of media which persists to this day, in spite of the close relation of film and photography, which can be compared to that of painting and sculpture. Among the classic films screened were *The Cabinet of Dr Caligari* (Robert Wiene, 1919), *Entr'acte* (Rene Clair, 1924), *Variety* (E. A. Dupont, 1925), *The Last Days of St Petersburg* (Vladimir Pudovkin, 1927), *Ten Days That Shook The World* (Sergei Eisenstein, 1927), *The Passion of Joan of Arc* (Carl Dreyer, 1928) *L'Etoile de Mer* (Man Ray, 1928), *The Circus* (Charles Chaplin, 1928), and *Man with a Movie Camera* (Dziga Vertov, 1928).

Thus the Deutsche Werkbund summed up the photographic contributions of the decade in a fashion not dissimilar to the International Exhibition of Pictorial Photography organized by the Photo-Secession in the Albright Art Gallery in Buffalo in 1910. Both of these exhibitions marked the end of a period. What is remarkable is that half a century later the selection of the photographers and their work by these two societies has withstood the test of time.

31. For an excellent report on the film festival, see A. Kraszna-Kraus, 'Exhibition in Stuttgart, June, 1929, and Its Effect,' *Close Up*, V, December, 1929, 455–64.

Herbert Molderings 1978

Urbanism and Technological Utopianism Thoughts on the photography of Neue Sachlichkeit and the Bauhaus

Paralysis and stagnation dominated international photography at the turn of the century; it was the result of a pervading crisis of development, both economic and aesthetic, in which old processes, conceptions, and forms were in their death throes and only faint, hesitant signs of new life were discernible. The replacement of time-consuming and quantitatively limited painting and drawing by technical pictures about 1840 had happened just at the right moment to meet the new scope of needs for information and entertainment in expanding a capitalist economy and society. The invention of photography had coincided with a period of a fully developed commodity production, and all successive developments of the photographic image took place as functions of its commodity character. Its exchange-value was based on a definite, constantly renewed intellectual and spiritual use-value, the essence of which consisted of bringing to people in pictorial form landscapes and cityscapes, monuments, personsages and events that in their lively and original form were not accessible to those people's aesthetic enjoyment. Photography, itself a commodity, steadily increased the range of commercial economy by bringing into circulation reproductions of objects that were not otherwise available. The stagnation that prevailed in the first two decades of this century was due to the fact that the first stage of this process had been completed while the next had not clearly taken shape.

About 1900 the whole visible world had already been reproduced into camera pictures. This spreading out of photographs was accompanied by a decline in the high aesthetic sensitivity, with which people originally viewed them. This illustrates the degree to which the effect of wear affects not only the usage of material objects, but also the social use of pictures and pictorial forms. Photography, which people had often examined with a magnifying glass in the first years of its existence had ceased to stimulate human attentiveness. A reaction to this stage of development was the so-called *Kunst-Photographie* which set the tone up into the twenties. It based itself on the clubs, magazines and exhibitions of the 'educated' photo-amateurs, which had come into being about 1890. Their main objective was to save photography from the loss of its cultural evaluation, by heaving it up onto the pedestal of fine art. They advocated a theoretical standpoint, which was characterized above all by its attempt to escape the accusation that photography was merely a mechanical recording process of material objects. With the aid of a soft-focus lens and special printing processes, they transformed photography into graphics, and tried to hide its particular traits and qualities by making its surface simulate a hand-drawn print. The largest part of 'pictorial photographic' production was a faint distant echo of Impressionism and the Secession-movement, which at that time had already played out their role in the development of art.

By bringing out the particular, technical possibilities of the photographic apparatus, which were superior to painting, a new generation of artists and photographers pitted itself against the prevailing practice of 'Kunst-Photographie' after World War I. The aesthetic renewal of the photographic craft, which it undertook and which by analogy with painting received the name

Erich Mendelsohn *Detroit — rear wall of a hotel*

of 'new realism' (*Neue Sachlichkeit*),[1] consisted not so much in discovering new areas of observation as in renewing or rediscovering what was already known by means of a change in photographic technique: an innovation in the method of reproduction. As Albert Renger-Patzsch, the chief representative of the new school, contended,[2] the task of photography was not simply to copy things but once more to explore and display them. This alteration of technique is also central to the principal artistic theory of photography at the time, advanced by the constructivist Laszlo Moholy-Nagy, who wrote in 1925 in *Malerei, Fotografie, Film*: '. . . the camera can perfect or supplement our own optical instrument, namely the eye. This principle has already been applied to various forms of scientific investigation, such as the study of movement (walking, jumping, galloping) and zoological, botanical and mineral forms (enlargement and microscopic views); but these were isolated experiments and their interconnection was not observed . . . So far we have only used the camera's potentialities in a secondary manner . . . This is also seen in so-called 'mistaken' shots – from above, below, or sideways – which already in casual photographs of today are impressive.'[3]

The new technique was naturally not an isolated autonomous development but was part of a complex of post-war social and aesthetic tendencies, which I would designate by the title of urbanism and technological utopianism. In recent years the liberal intelligentsia has turned away from both these concepts and has devoted itself to 'back to nature' and ecological perspectives.

Although industry and technology were the classic achievements of the bourgeoisie, they were denied a place in bourgeois art right up to the beginning of the twentieth century. Scarcely had photography been invented when it was subjected to an anti-technical artistic theory based on the superstition, that art could never originate as the result of a mechanical recording process, and could only occur outside of the social process of production. Such idealistic dogmas of the Wilhelmenian Reich were shattered on the battlefields of World War I and the November Revolution. The post war years witnessed a feverish search for new artistic perspectives; its most vivid expression was the experimental laboratory of Dadaism. Those who did not see the solution in terms of social revolution on the Russian model recognized it in the forced industrialization which characterized Germany during the Weimar Republique.

During the period of stabilization in Germany the liberal intelligentsia looked primarily towards America. With its superior technology and with the system of parliamentary democracy still functioning, in contrast to continental Europe, the USA appeared to intellectuals as the model of a future classless society, achieved without the social upheaval that had just taken place in Germany. Faith in America took on a religious quality: as one representative of the movement put it, 'We were determined to make the present honourable, and we were enthusiastic for the future. We held firmly by America. America was a good idea; it was the country of the future. It was at home in its own decade. We were too young to know it, but we loved it none the less. For long enough we had known the glorious discipline of technology only in the form of tanks, mines and blue cross gas, the destruction of human life. In America it was in the service of human life. We all felt a demonstrative enthusiasm for lifts, jazz and radio-towers.'[4] Erich Mendelsohn's photographs of architecture in his very popular

I am indebted to John Webb for his assistance with the translation of this essay.

1. See Wilheln Kästner, Photographie der Gegenwart, Grundsätzliches zur Ausstellung im Museum Folkwang Essen, in *Photographische Rundschau*, Heft 5, 1929, pp.93/94.
2. Albert Renger-Patzsch in *Fritz Kempe, Das Bild und die Wirklichkeit*, Grünwald 1974, p.46.
3. Laszlo Moholy-Nagy, *Malerei Fotografie Film*, München 1927, p.26.
4. Hans A. Joachim, Romane aus Amerika, in *Neue Rundschau*, 1930, II, p.398.

book *Amerika* (1926) gave symbolic expressions of these 'hopes of a new world'.[5]

On all sides there was heard a demand from one section of the intelligentsia that due honour should be paid to the industrial and technical aspects of reality, both in the subject-matter of art and as regards its media. At a time of passionate debate on the decadence of art and the means of saving it, many felt that photography, itself a child of scientific and technical progress, was the natural medium of expression of the 'industrial world'. 'Man in the industrial age seeks an appropriate expression of his cultural attitude towards the world. For decades he was hampered in this by tradition and by the feeling that he must subject himself to it, until a few years ago there arose the movement which derives new creative impulses from the possibilities of city life.' Thus wrote Karl Sommer in a review of the important international exhibition at Stuttgart, *Film und Foto 1929*, which contributed to the triumph of the new 'urban' vision.[6] By developing pictorial forms for this so-called 'new vision' (Moholy-Nagy), the photographer sought to raise his medium to the level of the general experience of the modern city-dweller, aiming at overcoming the contradiction between a past-oriented visual culture, and the contemporary day-to-day life dominated by industry and not by gods and fairies. One aspect of the new approach was the substitution of the vertical for the horizontal perspective. Views from lifts, radio towers, cranes, and aeroplanes endowed the world with the curious beauty of a diagram. An important manifesto of this vision was Eugen Diesel's *Das Land der Deutschen* (1931) a volume containing 481 reproductions of aerial photographs mostly by Robert Petschow, who had for 20 years been photographing the German landscape of 'nature, civilization and machines'[7] from balloons and zeppelins. The book was so popular that in 1933 the publishers decided to issue a cheap edition. Precipitous views from above were matched by soaring perspectives of skyscrapers. The whole environment was subjected to this new skyscraper perspective, even there, where people were confronted by it as a result of a completely different historical sensibility. The new photographers avoided totalities and confined themselves to detail. Sober functional forms displayed abstract beauty in severely restricted detail. It was the 'beauty of technology' *(Schönheit der Technik)*, title of a book by Franz Kollmann in 1928, for which the 'new vision' was essentially a search for.[8] Therefore the appropriate parallel in terms of painting is not really the 'new realism' but rather constructivism, a movement which combined a fervant belief in the effect of technology on social reform, with a predilection for unusual dynamic viewpoints which, it was hoped, would give the spectator an impression of the future. Some artists, in fact, were both 'new realist' photographers and constructivist painters, for instance Alice Lex, Werner Gräff, Herbert Bayer, Oskar Nerlinger and Laszlo Moholy-Nagy. *Bauhaus* photography and photography of *Neue Sachlichkeit* were two developments of one essential concept, as is demonstrated in Werner Gräff's book *Es kommt der neue Fotograf!* (Here Comes the New Photographer!) in 1929 as well as Renger Patzsch's *Die Welt ist schön* (1928).

The new style of photography appeared realistic to contemporaries in contrast to impressionistic art photography, the soft, 'soulful' technique of which was out of keeping with the hard, uncompromising surfaces of modern concrete, steel and glass. The 'soul' of technology was recognized to consist in the iron

5. Erich Mendelsohn, *Amerika, Bilderbuch eines Architekten*, Berlin 1926, IX.
6. Karl Sommer, Film und Foto, Ausstellung des Deutschen Werkbundes, in *Essener Allgemeine Zeitung*, 26 May 1929.
7. Eugen Diesel, *Das Land der Deutschen*, Leipzig 2, 1933, p.13.
8. See Albert Renger-Patzsch, *Eisen und Stahl*, Berlin 1930; *Technische Schönheit*. 64, Bilder, Zürich and Leipzig 1929; Rudolf Schwarz, *Wegweisung der Technik*, Potsdam (ca. 1930); *Das Werk. Technische Lichtbildstudien*. Köigstein im Taunus und Leipzig 1931.

laws of its construction. Photographers now began to look for similar patterns in all natural forms, in landscapes and in seascapes,[9] in stones and plants,[10] thus turning the world into an inexhaustible realm of abstract structures. Although Blossfeldt was a violent opponent of functionalist architecture, his photographs of plants reflect this trend, an emblem of which may be seen in the signet on the cover of Renger-Patzsch's *Die Welt ist schön*. This title 'The World is Beautiful', which tempted so many critics into summing up their review in a catchword before they had properly begun it, was not devised by Renger-Patzsch but by the publisher of the book, which was originally entitled 'Things' *(Die Dinge)*[11]: its purpose was to recapture an aesthetic experience of the everyday surroundings, based on the recognition of a single formal principle common to natural and man-made objects. In these pictures photography caught up with the pace of artistic evolution, namely in painting: the abstract ornament of the painters was complemented by the ornamentalisation of the objective world through the photographers.

Whereas industry and technology had so far been excluded from bourgeois art, things now went to the other extreme: there was a regular cult of technology, and every one of the new photographs is a symbol of it. A very contradictory symbol, it may be added: for the emphasis of photography on technical progress was matched by the social retrogression which was the price of that progress in the capitalist Weimar Republic. 'Enthusiasm for technology', the 'romance of engineering' and the 'cult of industry' are slogans that leave a bitter taste in the mouth, as technology was soon to find its most advanced embodiment in Fascist war industry.

In Russian photography, especially the work of its greatest innovator Alexander Rodchenko, very similar principles were in favour at the same period, a fact which illustrates the close relationship between photographic methods and the development of productive forces. In his article 'Ways of Contemporary Photography' (1928) Rodchenko emphasized the correlation between modern photography and urban-industrial conditions of life. 'Modern cities with their many-storey buildings, special factory installations, display windows reaching to a height of two or three storeys, trams, motor cars, luminous advertisements and neon signs, steamers, aeroplanes . . . all this has necessarily changed the customary psyche of visual perception. It is as though only the camera were able to depict life as it is today.'[12] From the point of view of social history the resemblance between Rodchenko's photographs and those of Renger-Patzsch or Moholy-Nagy is the effect of a temporary historical overlap. There is a danger here of thinking like an instaneous photograph, which freezes the unity of opposites, and which does not allow the different historical-cultural continuum of their origin to come into focus. Conditions in revolutionary Russia justified the hope that technical progress would henceforth be used for the benefit of humanity instead of pauperizing the greater part of it. The Russian revolution, which liberated all productive forces, also for a time liberated the art of photography, until it was gradually throttled as a result of Stalin's campaign against the 'left opposition' in art and the resolution of the Central Committee of the Soviet Communist Party of 23 April 1932, which forced the dissolution of the free photographic initiative-groups.

Economically the aesthetic renewal of Wilhelmenian, pre-war photography,

9. Arvid Gutschow, *See Sand Sonne,* Hamburg 1930.
10. Karl Blossfeldt, *Urformen der Kunst,* Berlin 1928, (2nd ed. 1929), *Wundergarten der Natur.* Berlin 1932; Ernst – Fuhrmann, *Die Pflanze als Lebewesen,* Frankfurt/Main 1930; Paul Wolff, *Formen des Lebens, Botanische Licht-bildstudien,* Königstein im Taunus und Leipzig 1931 (2nd ed. 1933).
11. See Albert Renger-Patzsch in Fritz Kempe (note 2).
12. Alexander Rodchenko in *Novyj LEF,* No.9, 1928, 31–39, quoted from *Alexander Rodtschenko, Fotografien 1920—1938,* Köln 1978, p.55.

which had fallen into sentimental mood pictures, was part of a fundamental reversal of the capitalistic system of communication, which took place after the end of the First World War. The 'photographic renaissance of that time had its material driving forces in the young commercial branches of *illustrated magazines* and *advertising*, which began rapidly expanding after 1918. A constantly growing market for information, and the competition among the leading illustrated magazines opened the way for experimentation and originality. Inventiveness and new methods were in demand, in order to revolutionize the advertising system, which was still functioning on a nineteenth century level, as an adaptation of trade to the monopolisation of production, which was growing in leaps and bounds. The book market supplied the third basis by bringing out the new artistic genre of the *photo-album*. These new economic perspectives of the photographic trade attracted numerous young creative people, who otherwise would have devoted themselves to the 'free' non-applied arts (and who, for the most part did so, before they became photographers). Since then the historical process has turned into its opposite, and photography today is as deeply affected by the decay and crisis of these branches of economy as, in the days of the Bauhaus and 'new realism', it was inspired by their growing importance.

If we consider the 'new vision' in the context of its economic and social functions, what the historical content of the notion of 'new realism' is, becomes clear. Along with heavy industry, the machine which was its substratum and the new architecture which was its result, 'neo-realist' photography discovered the world of industrial products, and showed itself as a component of the aesthetic of commodities in a double sense, affecting both production and distribution. Such photographers as Burchartz, Renger-Patzsch, Gorny, Zielke, Biermann and Finsler discovered that an industrial product develops its own particular aesthetic only when the serial principle, as the general basis of manufacture, becomes pronounced visible.

From then on, all photographs in the new style were dominated by the rhythm of standardized objects and the ornamental accumulation of identical shapes. This was certainly right as opposed to the reactionary horror of standardization and the outcry of craftsmen and big landowners against the 'levelling' effects of industry. But the real situation was more complicated. Pictures displaying the beauty of the assembly line lost their social force by virtue of the fact that the assembly-line system had just thrown millions of workers out of their jobs. The photo-montages of John Heartfield on the title pages of the *Arbeiter-Illustrierte Zeitung* (AIZ, founded in 1924), and the photo-essays in the magazine *Der Arbeiter-Fotograf* (The Worker Photographer) devoted themselves to the everyday life of these workers, to their social plight and political oppression. *Der Arbeiter-Fotograf* appeared from 1926–1932 from the *Neuer Deutscher Verlag* as the organ of the association of the worker photographers, which functioned as a large proletarian photo agency, in a time when Willi Münzenberg, the initiator of both magazines, was trying to prevent a boycott of the *AIZ* on the part of the bourgeois photo agencies such as Mauritius-photo, ufa-photo, Ecce-photo etc. Formally the pictures in *Der Arbeiter-Fotograf* demonstrated very little similarity to the points of view of the avantgarde.[13] The people who created these photographs knew not only the everyday industrial life, but also the great social differences in the distribution of industrial products, too well to be seduced by a perspective with the motto 'The World is Beautiful'.

Commodities also came to be shown from a different point of view, directly linked with the needs of advertising. The development of *Sachfotografie* – the

13. See *Der Arbeiter-Fotograf, Dokumente und Beiträge zur Arbeiterfotografie 1926—1932*, Köln 1977.

photographing of individual objects – is recognized as an important achievement of photography in the twenties, an extension of vision to which Wilhelm Kästner referred at the beginning of 1929 in a review of the international exhibition of contemporary photography at Essen. He wrote: 'This is also the explanation of the fact that landscape is unpopular nowadays and that simple objects predominate – especially objects of everyday use, preferably mass-produced and arranged simply in piles, as distinct from still lives. This marks the transition from free, purely artistic creation after the fashion of painting, to applied photography in the service of publicity.'[14] Objects hitherto regarded as without significance are made 'interesting' and surprising by multiple exploitation of the camera's technical possibilities, unusual perspectives, close-ups and deceptive partial views. In 1931 the New York Art Center put on an exhibition of 'Foreign Advertising Photography', organized by Abbott Kimball of the advertising firm of Lyddon, Hanford and Kimball. This is of particular interest as it was the first exhibition to cover the new trend in photography from the special viewpoint of advertising. In a review in the New York *Evening Post*, Margaret Breuning drew attention to an interesting difference between American and European advertising photography at that time: 'Our advertising tends to illustration, the use of the article is demonstrated by its happy users. Far more often, and to many of us more effectively, the foreign advertisement presents the article itself in some unusual character which gains for it a provocative, arresting interest . . . the articles themselves seized at some unexpected angle of contour, or mass, exaggerated, distorted, if you will, but given a witty, sophisticated accent instead of the usual stodgy, literal explanation'.[15] The advertising value of such photographs consists precisely in the fact that the objects are not presented functionally and contain a promise of mysterious meaning over and above their ordinary use-value: they take on a bizarre, unexpected appearance suggesting that they live lives of their own, independent of human beings. More than all the fauvist, cubist, and expressionist paintings, it was applied photography which modified and renewed the centuries-old genre of the still-life from the bottom up. It created the actual still-life of the twentieth century: pictorial expression of commodity fetishism.

Since about 1930 photography has been steadily gaining ground over the graphic arts as a medium of advertisement. Even where neo-realist and constructivist photography did not directly originate as a means of advertising, it displays an intrinsic affinity with it. 'Chaque angle nouveau multiplie le monde par lui-même,' as the French photographer Germaine Krull noted in the preface to her little book *Étude de nu*. The constant renewal of things from within is a structural principle of advertising as it is of neo-realist constructivist photography – a fact to which Benjamin alluded when he uttered the firm pronouncement that this photography has more to do with buying and selling objects than with discovering them. Thus it comes as no great surprise to learn that Kertesz's *Fork*, one of the best-known specimens of neo-realist photography, proved highly suitable as an advertisement for Bruckmann's cutlery.[16] The shock of surprise, originally occasioned by the sight of the wealth of forms revealed by scientific photography, was made to serve the merchant as part of the technique of seducing a customer.

Within a few years the pictorial structure of the 'new vision' was fully developed: clear, sharp and precise reproduction, shots from unusual angles,

14. Wilhelm Kästner, see note 1.
15. Margaret Breuning, Foreign Commercial Photographs Make Brilliant Showing, in *New York Evening Post*, 7 March 1931.
16. See *Die Dame*, Heft 4, Nov. 1929, p.72. The silverware industrialist Peter Bruckmann was President of the Deutscher Werkbund, which in its journal *Die Form* did much to promote the new style of photography.

Albert Renger-Patzsch *Suburban houses*

close-up or from a great distance, narrowly limited detail instead of an en-
semble, isolation of particular features, emphasis on material surface and abstract structure. All this contributed to an aesthetically fragmented perception,
less human than technical and mechanical in its effect. It is a question whether
this so-called 'photographic sight' has really developed and extended our
natural powers of vision and perception, as is repeatedly claimed, or whether it
has not blunted them. Carl Linfert, one of the few who resisted the photographic
euphoria of those years, remarked in 1931 on the occasion of the exhibition *Das
Lichtbild* at Essen: 'How seldom photographs tell us anything about the objects
they show! But what is transmitted as a message to the eye stares at us like a
fetish – especially since Renger-Patzsch, photographs have become thus frigh-
tening . . . The urge to look, to record all that one sees, is so feverish that, while
we grasp at everything, we end up holding nothing . . . The thing itself, however
concisely and exactly the camera perceives it, has less to say to us than ever.'[17]
Man and things are both under a spell which inhibits understanding: the effect is
one of reified sight, the content of which is no longer the real world so much as
the camera's artistic technique. In this confrontation, things and men are alike
speechless.

17. Carl Linfert, Das moderne Lichtbild, in *Frankfurter Zeitung*, 8 October 1931, 10.

Brian Stokoe 1978

Renger-Patzsch: New Realist Photographer

I

Albert Renger-Patzsch was born in Würzburg in 1897. He attended the classical Grammar School at Sonderhausen and the Kreuzschule in Dresden where he sat for the school certificate in 1916. He began photographing at the early age of 15 with cameras belonging to his father who was an enthusiastic amateur. After the First World War, during which he saw service in both the sappers and the trench-mortars, Renger-Patzsch studied chemistry at the technical college in Dresden. After having completed only half of his preliminary examinations he left to take up a position as head of the photographic department of the Folkwang Archive in Hagen, where he photographed mainly art and ethnographic objects.

His first exhibition took place in Bad Harzburg in 1925 and in the following year he published his first book, *Die Chorgestühl von Cappenburg* (The Choirstalls of Cappenburg). *Die Welt ist schön* (The World is Beautiful) was published by Kurt Wölff of Munich in 1928. It contained 100 reproductions and one edition included a prefatory essay by the then head of the Lübeck Museum, Carl Georg Heise. It is for this book in particular that Renger-Patzsch has been viewed as the father of modern European photography and originator of the *Neue Sachlichkeit* or New Realist style. What follows is an attempt to highlight certain issues arising both out of his work and the way in which it has been evaluated, issues which, since the 1920s at least, have largely remained uninvestigated.

II

According to Walter Benjamin the adoption of photography by the French State in 1839 provided the basis for a 'continually accelerating development which for a long period foreclosed all retrospective appraisal'[1], but of the many historical and philosophical questions left unattended in the twentieth century one in particular distinguishes itself: that of realism. The fact that a considerable amount of study during the last ten years has focused on this very question, especially in the realm of film theory, may or may not, depending on your point of view, 'be linked subterraneously with the crisis of capitalism'. Nevertheless the historical determination of its lengthy neglect can certainly be located in the early years of photography when, having neither an adequate conceptual framework nor suitable vocabulary, both public and pioneer grappled with the unique properties of the photographic image.

The excitement and astonishment with which the public announcement of the invention of photography was greeted would appear to have been largely informed by the belief that Man could now see his world as it *really* was. As direct successor to the Camera Obscura the photographic camera carried the impeccable credentials of an optical process; its images were made with real light, rendered as naturally as would be an animal track, and required neither knowledge of drawing nor any manual dexterity. It was on this same belief that the physicist François Arago based much of his famous and prophetic speech to the Académie des Sciences in August, 1839. Despite the attendance of members

1. Walter Benjamin, *A Short History of Photography*. Creative Camera International Yearbook, 1977, p.162.

of the Académie des Beaux-Arts the comparison with painting was unavoidable:

'The task of copying the millions and millions of hieroglyphics which cover even the exteriors of the monuments of Thebes, Memphis and Karnak etc., would require both many decades of work and a whole army of artists. With the Daguerreotype one man could successfully carry out this immense labour . . . and the drawings [sic] would surpass the works of the most accomplished painters in terms of both accuracy and local colour'.[2]

Numerous terms coined by the pioneers of photography were similarly founded – Niépce's *Héliographie* and Fox Talbot's *Pencil of Nature* for example – terms which, although instrumental in extolling the new invention's virtue as a natural and almost God-given process for the depiction of the world, implicitly dismissed the role of the human operator and prompted the notion of the photograph's objectivity. Fox Talbot wrote of his *View of the Boulevards at Paris,* 'A whole forest of chimneys borders the horizon: for instance, the instrument chronicles whatever it sees, and certainly would delineate a chimney-pot or a chimney-sweeper with the same impartiality as it would the Apollo of Belvedere'.[3]

Here in the nineteenth century we find some of the origins of the belief in the axiomatic truth of the photograph, the basis of the myth of an unmediated verisimilitude which not only lends the term *photographic realism* a distinctly tautological quality, but also makes any suggestion that this realism is somehow problematical resemble a cultural blasphemy of the first order. Photographs are seen to *re-present* reality, to stand for it. So much so that they 'do not seem to be statements about the world so much as pieces of it'.[4] The medium appears as a transparent window on the world through which we perceive an optically determined and therefore unbiased truth grounded in what appears to be an exclusively denoted image. As one of Renger-Patzsch's contemporaries put it, 'Photography avoids the literary or aesthetic importance of things. It is free of value judgement'.[5]

Much of the literature which has attempted an evaluation of Renger-Patzsch's work has been pervaded by this same 'natural' view of what constitutes realism. Put simply, the new realist label attached to his straightforward, 'sachlich' photographic approach has been secured by the juxtaposition of his work with that of the pictorialists who dominated the hierarchical structure of art photography. To such a purist as Renger-Patzsch their work smacked more of painting than photography, a pernicious confusion of means which set the photographer 'at odds with the veracity and unequivocal nature of his resources, materials and technique'.[6] However, this concept of realism has certain fundamental problems, not the least of which is that it cannot be used for any qualitative analysis of photorahic practice. The sharp-focus style characteristic of *Neue Sachlichkeit* imagery became, as we know, the minimum social and aesthetic requirement; moreover it was fast becoming so when Renger-Patzsch published his earliest work. Were we to follow this concept *reductio ad absurdum* we could do no other than allocate equal status to all photographs which manifest such peculiarly photographic qualities. Such a concept of realism would, of course, deny that interests contend in the world and refuse to acknowledge that photographs are manifestations of interest; still further, it would place the final seal of approval on an activity which unquestionably promotes the

2. François Arago, *Compte Rendu des séances de l'Académie des Sciences,* 1839, 2e Semestre. Meeting of Monday August 19, p.259. Translation by Brian Stokoe.
3. William H. Fox Talbot, *The Pencil of Nature.* 1844. Referring to plate II.
4. Susan Sontag, *Photography.* New York Review of Books, Oct. 18, 1973, p.59.
5. Hans Finsler, *My Way to Photography.* Pendo–Verlag, Zurich, 1971. Referring to image p.24.
6. Albert Renger-Patzsch, *Ziele.* Das Deutsche Lichtbild, 1927. Translation by Trevor Walmsley.

entire history of photography as a hermetic arena of study quite independent of the medium's social function. Yet however much the medium may seek to deny and render invisible its own terms it cannot escape them.

III

'if the new movement in the arts is going to produce a Utopia, that Utopia will be found in Germany. All the forward looking ideas, ideals, enthusiasms and tendencies of the century have found a home there . . . Germany has suddenly become endowed with an intense "modern consciousness" and looks forward more eagerly than other nations because it does not care to look back'.[7]

By 1929 there was indeed much that many Germans might not readily care to look back upon. They had suffered defeat in a war of unprecedented barbarity, their humiliation greatly exacerbated by the vicious terms of the Treaty of Versailles, and experienced both an abortive socialist revolution and installation of a liberal-democratic republic. The period from 1919 to 1923 was characterized by both internal violence and obduracy on the part of the Allies regarding war reparations. In January 1923 Franco-Belgian troops occupied the Ruhrland and by October inflation had reached the fantastic proportions for which this period is renowned; taking advantage of the uncertain state of affairs Hitler and Ludendorff planned an unsucessful *coup d'état* in Munich.

But the optimism at the heart of William Gaunt's assessment was not without foundation. The French elections of May 1924 had removed Raymond Poincaré, and his successor Edouard Herriot proved less intransigent regarding the enforcement of Versailles. Troops were withdrawn from the Ruhrland in 1925 and foreign aid made available for the reconstruction of industry and modernization of plant. The period from 1925 until the Wall Street crash in the autumn of 1929 was one of relative economic and political stability in which the republic appeared to be strengthening its powers of resistance.

However, not everyone expressed either such confidence or enthusiasm in the onset of a technological Utopia. The playwright Gerhart Hauptmann envisaged a 'waste world' the arrival of which would inevitably spell the destruction of the German soul: '. . . when American steel structures have replaced the last Romanesque, the last Gothic, and the last Renaissance building, secular or sacred, then indeed will everything have perished that with throbbing heart we now call Germany'.[8]

This antagonism between modernism and tradition, between a forward-looking optimism and a melancholic longing for an apparently disappearing world, was much to the fore in photographic book production during the 1920's. Hauptmann's remarks occur in an introductory essay to Kurt Hielscher's *Deutschland* published in 1924 as one of the Orbis Terrarum series. Hielscher pictured a land untouched by the 'prosaic spirit of mere utility' and constituted almost entirely of austere Gothic architecture. The images were reproduced on matt surface paper with sepia inks which lend them an atmospheric and evocative quality; they presented a view of Germany to which one could perhaps only respond affirmatively by making the required comparison with some fallen state of urbanization at which the country was supposed to have arrived. Hauptmann's stress on spirituality was also crucially important for art photographers of the period, for when combined with an anti-technical notion of art it provided the legitimization for those techniques so disdained by Renger-Patzsch. Writing in the annual *Das Deutsche Lichtbild* in 1927 Karl von Schintling sought to maintain a position that was by this time becoming somewhat unfashionable: 'Only that which the creative artist contributes from within himself . . . makes

7. William Gaunt, *A Modern Utopia?* The Studio, Dec. 1929, pp.859–65.
8. Gerhart Hauptmann, prefatory note to *Deutschland* by Kurt Hielscher, 1924. English ed. *Picturesque Germany*. T. Fisher Unwin, London.

a mere likeness into a work of pictorial art. It should not therefore be necessary when speaking of artistic photography to justify what is described as 'interference', because without such interference with the inevitable chemical and mechanical processes . . . it is inconceivable that one could influence the picture in the sense of transforming it in an artistically substantial way'.[9]

It was in this same edition that Renger-Patzsch expressed his views on photography. In an article entitled *Aims* he presented an opinion completely at variance with that of von Schintling and argued for adherence to the basic optical and mechanical properties of the medium: 'The secret of good photography, which can possess artistic qualities . . . lies in its realism. Let us therefore leave art to artists and let us attempt, with the resources available to photography, to create photographs which can endure thanks to their photographic qualities, without us having to borrow anything from art'. However, this concept of realism was, for Renger-Patzsch, inextricably bound up with the change in subject matter both required and made available by an advanced industrial society. Photography's inherent characteristics made it the only process which could 'do justice in pictorial terms to the rigid lines of modern technology, the spacious interwoven girderwork of cranes and bridges, and the dynamics of one thousand horse-power machines'. The pictorialist argument that the camera reproduced form in a mechanical and therefore unartistic way made it, 'in these instances, superior to all other means of expression'.

Modernist photography was used to lend support to the same Utopianism expressed by William Gaunt: 'Industry in itself is astounding anyway, but the Germans deliberately dramatize it to make it still more so, and the factory and the shop are designed not only in the most enlightened way for use, but also to strike the imagination and to suggest power'.[10] It provided the ideal technique for the totemization of new industrialial structures and artifacts by presenting them in 'abstract' diagrammatic form.

In *Die Welt ist schön* this technique was applied to a spectrum of subject matter ranging from people and plant life to industrial materials and buildings. Whereas other adherents to this approach had restricted themselves to rather specialized fields, 'Renger-Patzsch's camera covered them all. His importance lies in the fact that he was not only the *first to conceive* a new ideology in European photography, but also the first to apply it to *everything* his eye spotted as worth photographing at all'.[11] However, the less utterable fact is that it was an 'ideology' which promoted the cultivation of photographic *seeing* completely independent of either what was being seen or was worth seeing. A technique whereby reality is appropriated for photographic ends and made to deliver up an apparently endless array of agreeable and supposedly meaningful compositions. Such an activity is far more likely to alienate the photographer from the world than engender unity with it. It was, as one critic has put it, a technique which 'lifts the image above the banality of the subject matter and moves it into a world of mystery and reticence'.[12] But notions of mystery are hardly congruent with a purportedly realist technique, the two are antithetical.

The beautiful world of *Die Welt ist schön* is only attainable by an aestheticizing tendency which, completely content with the pictorial surface of things, suppresses the social milieu in which commodities and people both exist and function. 'Therein is unmasked a photography which is able to relate a tin of canned food to the universe, yet cannot grasp a single one of the human connections in which that tin exists'.[13] Within such terms things were 'neither

9. Karl von Schintling, *Lichtbildkunst*. Das Deutsche Lichtbild, 1927. Translation by Trevor Walmsley.
10. William Gaunt, ibid.
11. Helmut Gernsheim, in a letter to the author, March 10, 1978.
12. Klaus Jürgen Sembach, *Style 1930*. Universe Books, New York 1971, p.19.
13. Walter Benjamin, ibid, p.232.

ugly nor beautiful, what is needed is to tear out the beauty hidden within them
. . . There is nothing which cannot be made beautiful'.[14] Even misery could be
transformed by the camera's cathartic eye. In what must surely be one of the
most bizarre pieces on photography ever written, Carl Georg Heise revealed the
true nature of this 'realist' technique:
    'A rear view of bleak houses in the suburbs, a still-life of roofs and chimneys,
involves more than a simple portrayal of buildings, and represents more than a
characteristic picture of the misery of the cultural waste-land which the city
dweller must face – transferring what has been observed from everyday reality
onto a black and white surface causes us to seek out interesting stimuli which we
had previously passed by without noticing'.[15]

Die Welt ist schö reduced the world to an inventory of objects and people
seen as objects, a reified and an historical view suggesting an order and harmony
the existence of which nascent Fascism was soon to disprove. Walter Benjamin's
comments on this book, in his seminal essay *The Author as Producer,* seem all
the more momentous if one remembers that his words were originally delivered
to the Institute for the Study of Fascism, in Paris. Momentous because, as even a
cursory glance at post-1933 editions of *Das Deutsche Lichtbild* will prove, the
techniques pioneered by Renger-Patzsch were well suited to providing equally
'realistic' pictures of Stormtroopers and Nazi Military hardware.

14. Carl Georg Heise, prefatory essay to *Die Welt ist schön,* Kurt Wölff, Munich, 1928, p.14. Translation by Trevor Walmsley.
15. Carl Georg Heise, ibid. pp.12–13.

Nummer 2. 11. Januar 1931.

Berliner

40. Jahrgang. Preis 20 Pfennig.

Illuſtrirte Zeitung

Derlag Ullſtein Berlin SW 68

Zeitgeſtalten VIII: Die Skiläuferin.
Auf dem Gipfel in der brennenden Winterſonne.

Bildnis „Leni Riefenſtahl"
von Martin Munkácsi

Cover of *Berliner Illustrirte Zeitung* 11 January 1931. Photograph by Martin Munkacsi of Leni Riefenstahl in *The White Hell of Piz Palu.*

Ute Eskildsen 1978

Photography and the Neue Sachlichkeit Movement

Neue Sachlichkeit was a phrase adopted in the 1920s to describe the realistic tendencies of a number of contemporary painters. The ideology itself was not confined to artists and to some extent was paralleled by developments in photography. The ways in which the concept of 'new objectivity' was defined by a camera were naturally linked to the photographic tradition and to the properties of the instrument itself, although much of the creative impetus came from other media, particularly Russian film. One must also remember that a photographic image always represents a piece of the real world; an 'objective' character is inherent in the medium.

During the period of intensive upheaval following the First World War, there was a specific desire for investigative documents, permanent records and a media which reached a mass audience. The camera was adopted as an important tool in a number of professions, particularly architecture, city planning, industrial design and experimental science. These professions, and marketing in general, fostered a steady demand for photographic commissions which were administered mainly by the press agencies responsible for producing brochures, magazines, and advertisements. As the majority of 'fine art' photographers were engaged in this work, it is just as important to consider the requirements of the 'brief', as it is to assess their originality *vis à vis* their aesthetic style. At the same time one is reminded that the photographers were not cut off from what happened before the war. They appreciated the efforts of photographers like Kühn, Demachy, Käsebier and Hoppé who had fought for the recognition of photography as a serious art form.[1] What they were opposed to was the so-called Pictorial photography in which the photographers imitated the sketchy, impressionistic view of period painters and relied on anecdote and voluminous atmosphere to win popularity in the annual salons.

This exhibition shows a selection of photographers who worked in the various fields named above. Beyond the expanded application of the medium, a functional principle can be seen developing in two main photographic directions: first the use of the camera as a mechanical instrument in a 'realistic' manner, and secondly the use of the machine as a resource for new visionary perspectives. The first, inspired by Albert Renger-Patzsch, stressed the object in the form which most eloquently expressed its structure, and used the medium to give this maximum emphasis. The second, advocated by Moholy-Nagy, emphasized the medium itself, and its dependence on light, as a means of extending our perception. Both are based on a principle of truth to the medium and, indeed, this could be used a synonym for 'the ideology of objectivity' in relation to photography. From this basis, an abstract realism developed on the one hand; and, on the other, a realistic photography for the mass media – realistic, that is, in its concern with aspects of contemporary, social life.

A growing political awareness – similar to the formation of groups among painters who were discussing the social and political role of the artist – emerged in photography with the 'worker-photographers' *('Arbeiter-Fotograf)* movement. Other examples of this direction in photography were Alice Lex and

1. Albert Renger-Patzsch, 'The Photographische Korrespondenz', 63. Band, 1927, p.80.

Oskar Nerlinger, members of the 'ASSO' group, who endeavoured to turn their work with experimental photographic techniques to political purposes; and August Sander, who devised a system of categorizing 20th century man according to occupation and class. The most outstanding artist of that time, using photography for social and political purposes, was John Heartfield who exploited the medium to the full in his photomontages.

While an objective approach was also apparent in France (Eli Lotar, Roger Parry, Maurice Tabard, René Zuber) and the CSSR (Jaromir Funke, Jaroslav Rössler, Jindrich Styrsky),their conception of objectivity was less pervasive. Outside of Germany photographers adapted elements of Surrealism, and their results became more literary and descriptive.

The beginnings of the 'New Photography'

The early stages in the development of the 'New Photography' owe a great deal, especially as regards content and form, to the unconventional use of the medium by the Berlin members of Dada (John Heartfield, Georg Grosz, Hannah Höch and Raoul Hausmann), in whose photomontages individual photographs were removed from their original context and placed in a setting which gave them a totally new meaning. The photograph appears in the montage still as a document, but while taking away the original authenticity, an association with authenticity is needed in order to read the new meaning. While the Berlin Dada artists were concerned with realistic photography – in John Heartfield's case it was the starting point for his trenchant visual propaganda – the Parisian Dadaists were interested in the photogram produced 'without the camera'. In 1923, Tristan Tzara wrote of the photographs of Man Ray: 'Since everything which is called art was suffering from rheumatism, our photographer lit his 1,000W bulb and the photosensitive paper gradually absorbed the profound blackness of our consumer articles . . . the mechanical, uniquely precise and exact dissolution of form is fixed, every line clarified, like hair seen through a comb of light'.[2]

Both methods, photomontage and photogram, illustrate the principle of simultaneity, a link with the concerns of Cubism and Futurism.

In 1931 Raoul Hausmann described the development of photomontage, commenting on its application, 'In contrast to earlier periods, the technique of photomontage has become much simpler. It was in part forced into such simpler modes due to the naturally evolving practical applications. The necessarily unequivocal political and historical slogans will always affect photomontage, thus removing it from the realm of initially individualistic playfulness'.[3]

Renger-Patzsch and Moholy-Nagy

'Art' photography prevailed in German photographic magazines, annuals and exhibitions until about 1929. The photographers who gave up doing 'fine prints' were now using gaslight and bromsilver paper with special colours and surfaces developed by this growing new industry. As late as 1930, the *Deutsche Lichtbild* (the photography annual) illustrated bromoil and pigmented emulsion prints and indirect advertisements for different types of paper such as gravure, carbon and volotype. In the magazines of other countries, in the mid and late 1920s, there are page after page of soft-focus, 'atmospheric' still-lifes, portraits and genre scenes.

However, the 'New Photography' was already being promoted in the first, 1927, issue of *Deutsche Lichtbild* with both Albert Renger-Patzsch and Moholy-Nagy expounding their concept of the 'new' medium. They singled out

2. Tristan Tzara, 'Man Ray und die Photographie von der Kehrseite', *Kunstblatt*, 1925, vol.9, p.230.
3. Raoul Hausman, 'a bis z', 16, 2. Folge, vol.10, p.61, 1931.

photography as an autonomous branch of art with its own particular qualities. Moholy-Nagy placed photography within the general field of the visual arts, but accorded it a special place by virtue of its light sensitivity. It was in this 'experimental' aspect that he was especially interested. By contrast, Renger-Patzsch related the medium to the concept of realism. He wrote: 'The secret of a good photograph – which, like a work of art, can have aesthetic qualities – is its realism . . . Let us therefore leave art to artists and endeavour to create, with the means peculiar to photography and without borrowing from art, photographs which will last because of their photographic qualities'.[4]

This idealistic concept of realism was already present in Renger-Patzsch's 1924 book on photographing flowers, *Das Photographieren von Blüten*. In this, Nature was taken as the model for beauty – a notion which he later extended to utilitarian objects and industrial products. He described reality in terms which are almost metaphysical, attributing to photography an extension of our vision and understanding because with its help we are able to perceive aspects of the natural world which are inaccessible to the naked eye. 'The excitement of this experience is that in taking a photograph, the eye has to adjust to the relatively small organism represented by a flower; it must see, as it were, through the eyes of the insects, and view their world as they do. We are amazed by the degree of perfection of structure, shape and colour. We recognize the basic elements of form out of which the style of different peoples has developed, and we sense unchanging laws, so fixed that they cannot be expressed in rational terms'.[5] An important element in Renger-Patzsch's view of Nature was his fascination with scientific illustration of detail. He used this method of examining structure in his own work. Through the omission of any reference to context, the formal appearance of objects was particularly stressed. His advice to the serious amateur was not to be content with mere technical facility but to consider the question of artistic form if he wanted his photographs to stand out from the ordinary.[6] With his dual concerns for photographic technique and aesthetic quality, Renger-Patzsch's intention was to capture 'the magic of the material world and the uniqueness of structure', and he considered photography the medium most suited to this purpose.

In 1925, when G. F. Hartlaub, Director of the Mannheim Kunsthalle, opened the *Malerei der Neuen Sachlichkeit* exhibition, which gave the movement its name, Laszlo Moholy-Nagy's book, *Malerei Fotografie Film,* was being advertised in the list of Bauhaus publications.[7] At this time, Moholy-Nagy was head of the Department of Metalwork at the Bauhaus, and he and his wife Lucia had been experimenting for three years with photography, especially with the photogram. This, despite the fact that as late as 1926 there was no photography course in the school and in the foundation course 'any instruction related to photography was unknown'.[8] In his chapter 'The Future of Photographic Techniques', Moholy-Nagy was optimistic about the new optical possibilities: 'When the true qualities of photography are recognized, the process of representation by mechanical means will be brought to a level of perfection never before reached. Modern illustrated magazines are still lagging behind, considering their enormous potential! And to think what they could and must achieve in the field of education and culture'.[9]

Moholy-Nagy formulated the specific characteristics of the photographic medium and, on this basis, proposed guidelines for its future practice. For him,

4. Albert Renger-Patzsch, 'Ziele', *Das Deutsche Lichtbild*, 1927, p.18.
5. Albert Renger-Patzsch, 'Das Photographieren von Blüten', *Kamera-Almanach*, 1924, pp.105–6.
6. Albert Renger-Patzsch, 'Photographische Studien im Pflanzenriech', op. cit., p.137.
7. Laszlo Moholy-Nagy, *Malerei Fotografie Film*, Bauhaus-bücher Band 8, Albert Langen, Munich, 1927.
8. Lux Feininger, *Interview Feininger-Eskildsen*, Cambridge, 1977.
9. Laszlo Moholy-Nagy, op. cit., p.32.

the medium itself was the content, but content was to be understood in terms of the extension of the boundaries of our perception. In the illustrations to his book, he juxtaposed a wide range of photographs without giving any information about their original context. The captions to the pictures only rarely illustrate his argument directly – for example, that accompanying the picture 'Sand' reads: 'What was once thought to be distortion is now an amazing experience, a challenge to re-evaluate the way we see. This picture can be looked at from any angle. It always presents a different view'.[10] Although these texts reflect his fascination with new ways of looking at things, they are often emotive as interpretations – for example, the following caption to Renger-Patzsch's photograph: *'Industrieschornstein-Animalisch wirkende Kraft eines Fabrikschornsteins'* (Factory chimney which reminds us of the power of animal forms).[11]

Form in nature and form in art

Comparison between form in Nature and in Art was a commonplace of discussions on photography in the 1920s. The documentary character of the photograph led to comparisons between structure in nature and artistic composition. Blossfeldt's photographs for example, were shown in the popular magazine *Uhu*[12] beside works of architecture and the other arts. Rudolf von Delius defined Nature as an aesthetically creative force: 'A self-generating will to form, governing and directing organisms, must be recognized as a fact'.[13] His article is illustrated with photographs of sea shells.

The emphasis on the appropriation of elements of external reality in Neue Sachlichkeit photography amounted to an ideal of objectivity; and yet the concentration on nature and on manufactured commodities indicates more an expansion of the traditional position to cope with a changing material world. Industry increased the number of new artifacts for the photographer to consider, but since these products were discussed in terms of 'the beauty of technology' and 'the engineer as the creator of new forms', the way in which they were seen was conditioned by the same attitudes. On the one hand, nature functioned as a compensating factor; on the other, in matters of design, as a model for the functional.

Form 'without ornament, with no trace of the old decorative aesthetic' had already been advocated by Hermann Muthesius in 1904. His challenging question, 'Is not an unadorned ocean liner an invention worthy of aesthetic contemplation?'[14], was only taken up in the 1920s when European and American photographers like Hans Finsler, Anton Bruehl, Johan Hagemeyer, Eli Lotar, Laszlo Moholy-Nagy, Will Keiling and Charles Sheeler became fascinated by the functional architecture of ocean liners. In 1929, Fritz Block took a series of photographs of this specific subject and used it as a basis for a technical analysis of form. 'The abstract research of the natural sciences found its way into technology by means of biogenetics. The popularization of scientific discoveries, together with the fashionable concepts of 'objectivity' and 'the functional', resulted in new forms of technical expression.'[15]

When Muthesius wrote in 1904 of the necessity of bringing machine products into the realm of aesthetics, he was reacting against the prevailing aesthetic which was anti-technological. His solution to this problem may be summed up in the motto of the German *Werkbund:* 'For the improvement of the products of

10. Ibid., 59.
11. Ibid., 57.
12. Robert Breuer, 'Grüne Architektur', *Uhu*, 1926, 2nd series, ol.39, pp.28–39.
13. Rudolf von Delius, 'Kunstform und Naturform', *Die Form*, 1st series, 1925, p.110
14. Hermann Muthesius, 'Umbildung unserer Anschauungen', *Kultur und Kunst*, Jena and Leipzig, 1904, 64.
15. Dr. Fritz Block, 'Versuche zur technischen Formanalyse', *Die Form*, 4th series, 1929.

manufacture'. Whether these turn of the century efforts at reform were also directed towards future social utopias is dealt with by Chup Friemert in relation to Muthesius' reference to the 'Taylor System' in America[16] and to other efforts to maximize productivity without concern for the people of the time: 'These views, to this extent, are an early form of that enthusiasm for technology which so possessed large numbers of designers and artists in the 1920s'.[17]

Two books which appeared in 1928, *Urformen der Kunst* (Prototypes of Art) by Blossfeldt and *Die Welt ist schön* (The World is Beautiful) by Renger-Patzsch – the latter was originally to be called *Die Dinge* (Objects). Both exemplify a structural view of the world and it is interesting to note that Blossfeldt used their pictures in his teaching. Indeed, Blossfeldt's specific use of the medium – illustrating a subject systematically in close-up and endowing it with a 'reality' unattainable to the naked eye – is relevant here. In *Die Welt ist schön*, Renger-Patzsch juxtaposed natural and industrial objects without commentary, thus showing the beauty of both and their similarities. His was a formal approach intended to equate subject and content through a systematic series of comparisons.[18] When asked about it in 1937, he described his book 'as an alphabet, intended to demonstrate how pictorial problems can be solved by purely photographic means'.[19] The text of the book underlines this. In it Carl Georg Heise put forward the idea of 'a revolution in aesthetic experience.'[20] Revolution, he went on to say, meant for him 'a reformation of the very foundations of aesthetics'. He ascribed a special quality to Renger-Patzsch's pictures, a 'hidden, secret, beauty', and remarked of a photograph advertising coffee that 'the coffee beans can be lingeringly savoured with the eyes of a connoisseur, as hard and black and smooth . . .'[21] Heise's words are characteristic of Neue Sachlichkeit and their public. Susan Sontag sees this tendency towards the aesthetic as something basic to photography: 'The camera alters the act of seeing itself, in that it encourages seeing for the sake of seeing'.[22] Heise considered it significant that Renger-Patzsch was not a portrait photographer: 'After all, aren't animals more interesting than people?'.[23]

The photography of August Sander

As already mentioned, August Sander began his documentary series on '20th century people' in the early 1920s at the same time as he was working as a commercial photographer on industrial and architectural subjects and portraits. Of the works which have so far been published and exhibited, we can identify his working method in which people are categorized according to profession and class. Other areas of his interest – for example, the images dealing, with facial detail – remain in negative. Sander research is still at an early stage and much under the influence of *Menschen ohne Maske* (Men without Masks), the book published by his son in 1971.

For Sander, photography was the most appropriate means for creating a documentary record of his time. In the context of the 'New Photography', he is

16. 'That the worker's spiritual nature is being appealed to is shown, for example, in the Taylor System established in America, whereby apathy at work is eliminated. The interested worker will develop a high degree of participation, and even a love for his machine, such as train-drivers have for their trains.' Quoted by Chup Friemert in 'Der Deutsche Werkbund als Agentur der Warenästhetik in der aufstiegsphase des deutschen Imperialismus', *Warenästhetik, Beiträge zur Diskussion, Weiterentwicklung und Vermittlung ihrer Kritik*, ed. W. F. Haug, Frankfurt, 1975.
17. Ibid., p.222.
18. Thomas Mann, 'Die Welt ist schön', *Berliner Illustrierte Zeitung*, 23 December 1928. Having lamented the influence of technology on art, he concludes with the question: 'But if the spiritual values are to find their proper place in technology, what if the reverse happens?'
19. Albert Renger-Patzsch, *Meister der Kameraerzählen*, Wilhelm Schöppe, Halle/Saale, 1937, p.48.
20. Carl Georg Heise, introduction to *Die Welt is schön*, Albert Renger-Patzsch, Leipzig, 1928, p.7.
21. Ibid., 11
22. Susan Sonntag, *Über Fotografie*, Hauser, Vunich, 1978, p.89.
23. Albert Renger-Patzsch, *Die Welt ist schön*, Leipzig, 1928, p.8

something of an outsider. For him, the essential importance of the photograph was its documentary character – an idea shared to some extent by others. However, Sander's documentation extended to a systematic analysis of man in his social context. His work on this project was carried out amongst the group of artists associated with the 'Cologne Progressives', and he was especially friendly with Franz Seiwert.

The ideas behind Sander's wide-ranging archive of portraits made a fixed format necessary as a basis for visual comparison. Some of the principal features of his method are: 1. the subject deliberately confronted with the camera and therefore given an opportunity to adopt a pose; 2. the subject always shown in the environment of his work, or life situation; 3. the subject generally shown full-length, usually in a serious mood. Sander's photographs show us people in various environments which for the most part relate to their particular social group. Nevertheless, their roles become fully recognizable only through their relationship to all the other portraits. His book *Antlitz der Zeit* (The Face of our Time) appeared in 1929 and forty-five more portfolios of twelve pictures each were planned. But these plans came to nothing and after the remaining part of the edition was seized by the Nazis, Sander devoted himself increasingly to landscape photography.

Alfred Döblin, who wrote the text for *Antlitz der Zeit*, likened Sander's method to that of comparative anatomy: 'In the same way, this photographer has practised comparative photography and attained to a scientific method far beyond the reach of the ordinary photograph'.[24]

The public reception of the 'New Photography'

From 1928, articles on stylistic problems in 'objective' photography increased in amateur and professional periodicals, and more attention was paid to the medium in the art journals.

As late as 1929, the photography critic, Willi Warstatt, emphasized the influence of Moholy-Nagy on the development of 'objective' photography particularly as a result of the book which Moholy-Nagy had published in 1925.[25] H. Wieynck made comparisons between Neue Sachlichkeit painting and photography in a lecture to the Photographic Society of Dresden. He declared himself sceptical of Franz Roh's suggestion that 'photographs be taken from nature, enlarged to the required size, coloured, and presented as works of art', and also of Wilhelm Worringer's appraisal of 'photographic accuracy' in contemporary painting. He affirmed the reversed roles of the two media: 'photography, generally speaking, no longer imitates art, rather art imitates photography'.[26] In this context, Wieynck saw no future for art as the recorder of physical appearances, though he went on to say that photography must not be allowed to rest on mere technical achievements, and put forward ideas for its 'creative' development.

The problem which predominates in these writings is that of determining which aesthetic factors are applicable to photography. The terms used ('the essence of things', 'pictorial construction', 'appropriate procedures', 'rules of style', 'form and expression', 'the artistic image') combine ideas inherited from 'art' photography with an improved understanding of the possibilities arising from technical developments. There is a desire to base a photographic aesthetic on technical factors, but at the same time a resistance to any loss of personal freedom in picture-making.

24. Alfred Döblin, *Antlitz der Zeit*, Transmare, Munich, 1929, p.14
25. Willi Warstatt, 'Die entfesselte Kamera und die produktive Kamera', *Deutscher Kamera-Almanach*, 1929, vol.19, p.44.
26. H. Wieynck, 'Die künstlerische Bildgestaltung in der Photographie', *Photographische Rundschau*, 1926, p.227.

106

Two attitudes prevailed: on the one hand, technical considerations were regarded as important in so far as they helped capture the essential character ('reality') of the subject; and, on the other, they were thought to be the basis for 'a new way of seeing' in which the camera's vision became the subject of the photograph. Common to both was the fact that any discussion of what was represented and how it was represented – that is, an evaluation of form in terms of content – was avoided. Siegfried Kracauer wrote on this problem in 1927: 'In order for the subject to be meaningfully represented, the mere surfaces offered by the photograph must somehow be disrupted . . . the likeness achieved by the photograph refers only to the exterior of the object, which does not readily disclose its internal meaning as it manifests itself to the understanding'.[27] In contrasting art with photography, Kracauer attributes to the former the ability to convey 'transparency'. His criticism is fair in respect of most of the adherents of the 'New Photography' in that their lack of awareness of a deeper reality and relative inexperience of the medium led to a fascinated preoccupation with unusual aspects of the physical world. But it is arguable that Kracauer failed to consider in photography, the series of reportage, that is its mechanical aspect, and hence simplified his discussion,

The affirmative attitude is exemplified in an essay of 1928 by Johannes Molzahn: '. . . the newspaper which brings you news of world events several hours later; the illustrated magazine – perhaps not today, but tomorrow – the same driving force propels them all. Photography! That greatest of all present-day scientific, chemo-technical miracles – this triumph, with all its enormous consequences! . . . the photograph as pacemaker of our time and our rate of development; the sheer number and succession of optical sensations demanding continual assimilation by the eye and the mind. The photograph will be one of the most effective weapons against intellectualization, against the mechanization of the spirit. Don't read any more! Look! will be the essential factor in questions of education. Don't read any more! Look! will be the key-note in the development of daily newspapers – already the newspaper is steadily increasing in importance . . . We need decisive visual image makers *(Regisseme der Optischen Gestalt),* men of the split-second, adaptable, and always ready to act'.[28]

The 'New Photography' in advertising

The 'abstract realism' of the 'New Photography' was based on a way of looking at reality in terms of structure. Photographic technique was used to emphasize the most characteristic appearance of the object as form. In this, the Neue Sachlichkeit photography drew attention to the medium itself by discovering unfamiliar aspects in familiar objects. The 'self-promoting aspect of a 'new photograph was recognized for its manipulative power and exploited in the context of the developing and expanding advertising and publishing industry.

In German advertising journals of the mid 1920s, the highly developed state of the publicity industry in the USA and the existence there of professional training in the subject was much discussed. B. W. Randolph of the New York University had stressed the important role of advertising in commerce and how American universities – Harvard, Columbia, Chicago etc. – had taken note of this. 'We have a thoroughly specialized industrial production, and we must have thoroughly specialized methods of marketing'.[29] In 1925, the photographer and commercial artist, Max Burchartz, gave his definition of modern advertising: 'The essence of advertising consists of one will using every means of suggestion available to persuade the greatest possible number of other wills to act in

27. Siegfried Kracauer, 'Die Photographie', *Frankfurter Zeitung,* 28 October 1927.
28. Johannes Molzahn, 'Nicht mehr lesen! Sehen!', *Das Kunstblatt,* 1928, vol.12, pp.79–81.
29. B. W. Randolph, 'American Education in Advertising and Marketing', *Gebrauchsgraphik,* 1926, 3rd series, **2**, p.3.

determined ways . . . the expression of function necessitates a concept of design which informs the manufacturing process from the outset . . . good design organizes all the necessary parts into a balanced and harmonious unity.'[31]

The Neue Sachlichkeit photographer, with his mastery of photographic technique and his ability to select and frame reality in a telling manner, had an obvious role to play in the field of advertising. The new possibilities for manipulation opened up by the media and the photograph's apparent authenticity were the key factors underlying the extensive use of photography by the advertising profession.

Photo-journalism

Since 1923, a number of new magazines appeared on the market – *Münchner Illustrierte Presse, Kölnische Illustrierte, Weltspiegel, Das Magazin* etc. In this highly competitive profession, self-taught photo reporters like Felix H. Man, Erich Salomon, Alfred Eisenstaed, Martin Munkacsi and Wolfgang Weber soon led the field and by the end of the decade, two aspects of the new journalism had emerged as particularly important – novel subject matter and the picture story. The 'New Photographer' had to have a nose for the unusual since novelty was what was demanded in the bourgeois press: 'behind the scenes' items – the 'torture chamber of beauty', 'Ladies only', photographs taken secretly in court – are some typical examples. In the meantime, technical developments made it possible to work in extreme light conditions. The nightlife of cities became a

30. In this connection it should be noted that the relationship between the creative aspects of photography and its technical limitations was being discussed in the USA before 1920 by Alfred Stieglitz's circle. Here Paul Strand's article, 'Photography' (1916) and his semi-abstract photographs and street-scenes of the same period are particularly relevant. At the Clarence H. White School – founded in 1914 by White, who was a member of the Secession – an 'abstract realist' photography developed from 1910 onwards under the influence of the painter Max Weber. Among those graduating from the school at the beginning of the 1920s were the photographers Paul Outerbridge, Anton Bruehl, and Ralph Steiner. They immediately began working in the advertising and fashion trades.
31. Max Burcharts, 'Neuzeitliche Werbung', *Die Form*, 1925, vol.7, pp.138–9.

Berliner Illustrierte Zeitung No. 28, 12 July 1931. *The Academics' Hotel*
Photograph by Kurt Hübschmann

camera subject and the informal portrait superseded the studio portrait. The 'candid camera' approach was perfected in 1924 with the production of the Ermanox and the Ernostar objective lens with a speed of f/2. As early as 1925, a few photographers had changed to the Leica, invented by Oscar Barnak in 1913 and already in mass production. This camera was not only a more convenient size, but its use of perforated film made it possible to take a sequence of pictures. And with the development of picture-reporting beyond the single image to the picture-series, new forms of presentation became necessary. In turn this brought about a new division of labour – the final choice of pictures was left to an editor or picture editor.

When Walter Benjamin, discussing photography in the 1930s, concluded that the medium was becoming increasingly subtle and more modern, and that from then on no ordinary apartment block could be photographed without being glamourized in the process, he was also commenting on how refinement of presentation was replacing content itself. He went on with the plea: 'What we should demand of the photographer is the ability to place his picture in such a context that it cannot be read as a fashionable pictorial cliché, but is given some new, some revolutionary, meaning'.[32] Benjamin was presumably implying here that photographers should control the use of their work in the media, but at the time this would have required literally owning the media. Without such an assumption his plea looks naïve and fails to take account of the working conditions of photographers inside the publishing field.

The success of the picture story – championed by a few editors like Stefan Lorant, Berlin editor of the *Münchner Illustrierte Presse* – also led to more attention being paid to the individual photograph. From about 1929, the weeklies began to devote a special page to the 'New Photography'. Examples are shown under such captions as 'The Special Photo' or 'The Objective Photography of our Time'. At the same time when photography became an essential part of the mass media production the magazines acted as a showcase for the 'New Photography' and commercial photography took on a new aesthetic dimension.

The political propaganda

During the 1920s the particularly aggressive photo-journalistic practice of publications like *Arbeiter Illustrierte Zeitung* (AIZ) first began to develop. The AIZ emerged from the periodical *Sowjet-Russland im Bild*, which was founded in connection with the Workers International Relief. They were intended to inform the international proletariat about the famine in Soviet Russia and to get help (an order of Lenin).

Willi Münzenberg (Founder of the International Communist Youth) organized the WIR and ran the magazine which changed in 1922–3 to *Hammer und Sichel* and in 1925 to *Arbeiter Illustrierte Zeiting*. Münzenberg realized the possibilities of photography as a weapon for awakening the political consciousness of the proletariat. In 1926, he founded the *Der Arbeiter-Fotograf* as the publication of the Worker-Photographer movement. This arose from the AIZ's recognition that dependence on bourgeois picture agencies meant that it was not easy to get photos of proletarian life. So they turned to the workers themselves for photographs, one of the most remarkable achievements of the AIZ. In *Der Arbeiter-Fotograf,* encouragement and technical advice were provided and recent developments in bourgeois photography were discussed and criticized. An example of this was Walter Nettelbeck's criticism of the *Neue Sachlichkeit* photographers: 'Just as the petit-bourgeois tends to make radical leaps in the political sphere, so too in the field of photography. Now he divides the world into two different realities, one seen through human eyes, the other purely

32. Walter Benjamin, 'Der Autor als Produzent', *Versuche über Brecht*, Suhrkamp, 1975, p.107.

optical – just as long as we don't see the world as it really is!'.[33]The bourgeois photo-journals were reproached with striving after aesthetic effect, and this was interpreted as an inability to attain to 'any clear political view of the world.'

The AIZ staff, however, in comparison with the bourgeois press was very much conscious of the relationship of photographs to text, and they developed a synthesis with a highly propagandistic intent, the layouts were dynamic and often combined written documents, photographs, and drawings. This cannot be examined in detail here; suffice it to say that, for different subjects, according to their political importance, varying lay-outs and combinations of pictures and texts were evolved. And they recognized the effectiveness of photographs on the front page before John Heartfield became a permanent contributor in 1930 and designed his montage headlines. The last edition of the AIZ appeared in March 1933, after the Nazis seized power. Publication continued in Prague until 1938, under the new title *Die Volks-Illustrierte* from 1936.

The popularization of the medium

The picture book is of particular interest in the 1920s since it offered the possibility of dealing with themes in a more extended way than the scope of photo-journalism permitted. The variety of subjects published included landscape, townscape, architecture, industry and portraits of different peoples. The title of Renger-Patzsch's book *Die Welt ist schön* could also be used as the heading for a subject catalogue of such books. They differed little in format, usually one picture to a page, but there were significant differences in lay-out and typography. These variations are illustrated in the productions of two different publishers: the firm of Karl-Robert-Langewiesche in traditional style, and that of Klinkhardt & Biermann in the 'objective-modern' manner.

Publishers exploited the new interest in photography, in many cases simply publishing existing material. In 1930, Klinkhardt & Biermann started a 'photolibrary'. Their list for that year included monographs by Moholy-Nagy and Aenne Biermann, and announced as forthcoming titles: 'Police photos', 'Sports photos', 'Photomontage', and '100 years of nude photography'. Much attention was also paid to the new medium in the art and cultural periodicals of the time, an example being the article on 'Experimental photography' in No.3 of *Das Neue Frankfurt* in 1929.

There was a considerable number of photographic exhibitions in Germany in the mid 1920s. The Berlin *Kino- und Photo-Ausstellung* was largely devoted to the industry. The *Deutsche Photographische Ausstellung* which took place in the following year in Frankfurt was described in the press as the most comprehensive since the great Dresden exhibition of 1909.[34] This too was to a large extent a trade exhibition. The spectrum covered ranged from the historical photograph to the achievements of the carrier-pigeon! The exhibition catalogue indicates that 'art' photography predominated.

Only in 1928 was there a small exhibition of the 'New Photography': *Neue Wege der Photographie* (New Paths in Photography) was shown at the Kunstverein in Jena, and included work by Erfurth, Errell, Moholy-Nagy, Lucia Moholy, Peterhans, Renger-Patzsch, Reeck and Umbo. The exhibition also included material from the photographic department of the Prussian Ministry for Trade and Commerce, and from two private collections in Berlin. Pictures were divided into categories according to subject and intended use: portraits, nature photography, aerial and scientific photography, film-stills, photomontage, photograms, and advertisements. The division of an exhibition into such categories continued in Germany through the early 1930s, including the first

33. Walter Nettelbeck, 'Sinn und Unsinn der modernen Fotografie', *Arbeiterzfotograf,* 1929, vol.11, p.220.
34. *Die Form, 1926,* vol.12, p.275.

exhibition under the Nazi régime *Die Kamera* in 1933. The fact that museums began including anonymous photographs from the various applied fields was in itself an innovation and important in that it introduced a way of relating to photographs other than within the context of the retrospective show of an individual 'fine art' photographer.

The most comprehensive collection of photographic work of this period was the 1929 *Film und Foto* exhibition in Stuttgart, organized by the Deutsche Werkbund. This was a great public success – much helped by the accompanying publications, including such titles as 'Here Comes the New Photographer', 'Photo-Eye' and 'Film: enemies today, friends tomorrow'.[35] Franz Roh singled out for special attention the 'outsiders' who, through their uninhibited use of the medium, gave new blood to the conventional mannerisms of the professionals.[36] This exhibition was reviewed in amateur magazines as well as in newspapers and art journals.

In the same year, Renger-Patzsch reacted in a characteristic way to the increasing flood of pictures: 'The fashionable photograph, with a few exceptions, is a concoction of affectation and a feverish search for originality, combined with a total lack of any aesthetic standards or technical skill.' And he described the Stuttgart exhibition as 'an anthology of photographic one-day wonders in a pretentious setting'.[37]

Conclusion

The decisive scientific and technical discoveries, which affected the 1920s, date from before the First World War. However, their economic and social effects were not felt in Germany until about 1924, a time of rapid industrial growth and economic consolidation (when the Dawes plan became operative). After the previous fashion for idealization, with its concealment of technique, the photography in the 1920s celebrated the pervasive influence of technology through a new objective style. The altered relation to 'reality' of that time expressed itself as an optimistic belief in the technical possibilities of the medium, which in turn changed the mode of perception itself. Wolfgang Born's essay in 1929 illustrates how the ideals of Neue Sachlichkeit were shared by the exponents of the 'New Photography': 'This discovery of reality is the mission of photography . . . its essential nature is deeply in harmony with our present day concept of the world, its method of recording objectively is appropriate to the intellectual approach of a generation of engineers'.[38]

In looking at photographs of this period we have to remember that the image is at two removes from the spectator. There is the historical distance, with its implication of authenticity, and the formal aspect, determined by contemporary technical considerations. Beyond these considerations we have to take account of the new communicative values of a photography in the 1920s, which obliged the photographer to integrate this aspect into his work – the application affected the image production.

By the beginning of the 1930s, the photographer was firmly entrenched in the two specialized fields of advertising and photographic journalism. He was now master of all the technical and artistic means with which photography could be used to add weight to an idea. Thus, when the Nazis began to insinuate new

35. Werner Gräff, *As kommt der neue Fotograf!* Hermann Reckendorf, Berlin, 1929, Franz Roh, *foto-auge*, Ernst Wasmuth, Tübingen, 1929, Hans Richter, *Filmgegner von heute Filmfreunde von morgen*, Hermann Reckendorf, Berlin, 1929.

36. Franz Roh, 'Mechanismus und Ausdruck – Wesen un Wert der Fotografie', *foto-auge*, Ernst Wasmuth, Tübingen, 1973 (reprint), p.3.

37. Albert Renger-Patzsch, 'Hochkonjunktur', *Bauhaus No.4*, 1929, p.20.

38. Wolfgang Born, 'Photographische Weltanschauung', *Photographische Rundschau und Mitteilungen*, 1929, vol.7, p.141.

Erich Saloman *Summit meeting in Lugano* 1928
Chamberlain, Stresemann, Briand (and from behind) Scialoja

and perverted meanings into established forms, they found in photography a tool admirably suited to their purposes. The medium had enormously developed its potentialities during the Weimar period, and could now be absorbed by the Nazis for the greater effectiveness of their propaganda machine. The special issue of the *Berliner Illustrierte* on the 1 May 1933 which the Nazis called 'day of the national work' gives a convincing example of their sophisticated journalistic practice of the early 1930s which the Nazis could irritate.

39. Compare with the special issue of *Berliner Illustrierte Zeitung* of 1 May 1933 – photographs mostly by Martin Munkasci.

David Mellor 1978

London-Berlin-London: a cultural history The reception and influence of the New German Photography in Britain 1927–33

The British Cultural Context

On the invitation card for his 24th birthday party, in April 1929, Brian Howard, a British writer and convert to the new photography, printed a list of likes and dislikes in the arts. Besides, predictably, Cocteau and Diaghilev as heroes, he also nominated a range of influences emanating from Germany: Marie Wigman, Einstein, Spengler, Russian films and Grüenewald.[1] Similar images drawn from France were present, but heavily supplemented by a pronounced orientation towards Germany.

Howard's list was symptomatic of a re-orientation at the end of the 1920s away from French modernist culture as the primary point of reference for many British intellectuals and artists, and, instead, an inclination towards Germany. This was, in part, a reaction to Bloomsbury's consistent advocacy, through the 1910s and 1920s, of France as the sole home of modernism.[2]

The political background of the period further encouraged this tendency, for the *Entente Cordiale* had disintegrated in 1923 over the French occupation of the Ruhr and symnpathy was now extended to the Germans. The point of view prevailing in British government circles and among intellectuals was a wish for reconciliation with Germany. 'After 1919 the English less and less thought of Germany in terms of suspicion and power rivalry . . . the Weimar Republic was widely taken . . . as a splendidly successful new achievement of Liberalism.'[3]

The Poets encounter the New German Photography

Berlin, in particular, became the focus of a number of pilgrimages by young British writers: key figures like Brian Howard, W. H. Auden, Christopher Isherwood and Stephen Spender, who would mould the forms and tastes of the 1930s. Painters, too, came to Berlin: Francis Bacon in 1927, Wyndham Lewis and Wadsworth in 1930 and Glyn Philpott in 1931. For the writers and poets, contact with the new German photography and film was important, more perhaps, than for the painters. Their visits and stays coincided with the emergence of the new photography in its different guises – the severe Neue Sachlichkeit (New Objectivity), photo-journalism and the publication of the influential photobooks.

In this pattern Brian Howard was a forerunner; visiting Frankfurt and Berlin late in 1927, where he became a fanatical photographer. In the following spring he was '. . . obsessed with photography . . . it was as though no one had ever taken a photograph before . . .'[4] This enthusiasm for German photographic modes as a fundamental break, and opportunity to rechannel a primal vision, would be a response also found among professional photographers in Britain, three or four years later as they came to adopt the New Objectivity style.

Howard was to abandon photography after some collaborations with the London photo-portraitist Barbara Ker-Seymer around 1930, but Stephen Spender accorded photography a role of some significance in his writing. He admitted that photographs and films could be vital source material for poetry. He felt that Hoyningen-Huene's 'monumental studied poses'[5] suggested possibilities for a poet, and, like Isherwood, he proposed the 'photo-eye' as an

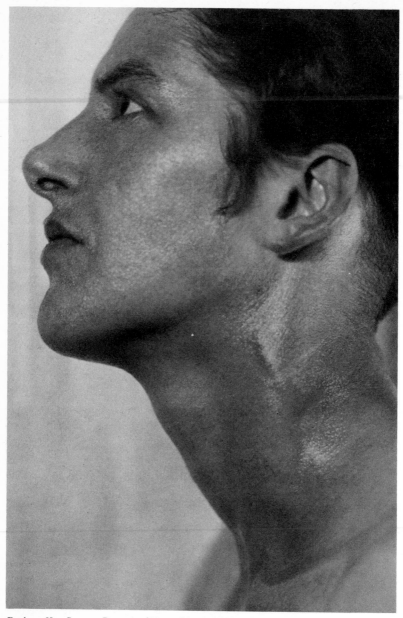

Barbara Ker-Seymer *Portrait of Nancy Morris* 1932

aesthetic. Spender admired Hoyningen-Huene's 'photographer's eye (resembling that of a German optical lens) for externals. This makes his work seem like the description of mechanical facsimiles rather than objects themselves'.[6] Here was the language of the New Objectivity spoken by an English voice. And the recurrence in Spender and Isherwood's writing of the camera or photo-eye could hardly be accidental, given the widespread interest in the photobook *foto-auge* (Photo-Eye) which commemorated the Stuttgart *Film und Foto* exhibition of 1929.

The Spender family were deeply enmeshed in the cultural network which supported the new German photography. Michael, the brother of Stephen and Humphrey, was an optician working in Germany for Leitz, the manufacturers of Leica cameras, at the end of the 1920s. The Leica's portability was a precondition of much of the informal photo-reportage of the time, and, around 1928, Michael advised Humphrey to ignore British cameras and purchase a Leica instead. Like Bert Hardy and a few others, Humphrey Spender was buying a way of seeing the world, bonding himself in the process to the new German photography.

It had been arranged that Humphrey should attend the Bauhaus at Dessau, and, in 1926–7 his family arranged for him to be introduced to Lucia Moholy, in London at the home of his grandmother, Frau Schuster. There, by extraordinary good fortune, he was shown Lucia Moholy's photographs which greatly intrigued him. However, when he eventually began his architectural studies in 1929, it was at Freiburg instead of Dessau and it was at this point that he became familiar, through the family with whom he lodged, with another element in the new photography – the photo-journalism of the *Münchener* and *Berliner Illustrierte,* as well as the Communist *Arbeiter Illustrierte Zeitung.*

Stephen and Humphrey were drawn towards the new photography, in the first place as amateurs, outsiders from poetry and architecture. Yet Franz Roh in his foreword to *foto-auge,* 'Mechanism and Expression', had commended such outsiders for coming into photography from other disciplines. Thus, Barbara Ker-Seymer became an experimental portraitist in the late 1920s with no training – '(I) didn't think of myself as a photographer'[7] – but she had a preference for printing sharply focussed, exact images; a preference which converged with the German New Objectivity sensibility in countering the prevalent misty and retouched portraiture of the 1920s. She also seems to have been the first London photographer to exploit negative printing consciously along the lines of Moholy-Nagy, in her *Portrait of Nancy Cunard* (1930–1). An outsider from sculpture – Barbara Hepworth – made a photogram self-portrait in 1932, stemming from Moholy-Nagy as well.

Certainly the Scottish writer, Kenneth Macpherson and his wife, Winifred Bryher, encountered photography from perspectives outside the profession. They began editing the film magazine, *Close Up,* in 1927, from Territet, in Switzerland, while Bryher also financed the literary magazine, *Life and Letters Today.* Like Brian Howard, Isherwood and Stephen Spender, their outlook was fundamentally literary (in the first issue of *Close Up* there were contributions from the Imagist poet H. D. and Gertrude Stein). It was a feature of some literary magazines – *transition,* was one of them – to publish advanced photography. But Macpherson and Bryher moved from the milieu of the literary magazine to an all encompassing interest in film and photography, transforming *Close Up* into a vital channel for the transmission of the new German photography. 'We believe', wrote Oswell Blakeston, the vanguard film maker and photography critic, in *Close Up* in 1929 'that photography is an art closely allied to cinematography'.[8]

Film und Foto: the Moscow–Berlin–London Axis

At the end of the 1920s, film and photography in Germany were reckoned to be more than just adjacent technologies and cultural forms – they were seen to overlap and interact. This was also recognized in certain British vanguard circles. When Zwemmers, the London booksellers and outlet for the German photobooks, advertised *Photo-Eye* and *Es kommt der neue Fotograf!* early in 1930 they were offered under the rubric of 'Recent Film Books' – 'although not strictly speaking film books (they) have a vital interest for all who follow modern film technique'.[9] Film was, perhaps, the dominant medium. E. O. Hoppé, who worked frequently in Germany during this period had come to believe so by 1933; 'In fact', he wrote, 'the movies have saved photography in spite of itself'.[10] Even F. J. Mortimer, the conservative Pictorialist, considered that the new photography was 'seeking for new standpoints and eccentric view angles, in some cases suggested by those exploited by modern cinema producers'.[11] If film now occupied a determining position, it was particularly the Soviet films of Eisenstein and Pudovkin that impressed German photographers, 'it shook them to the core'.[12] While British advertisers were being given a first description of the new German photography by Errell, in 1929, he attested that; 'The Russians revealed to us a new technique of composition'.[13] Within a year the British photographer Gilbert Cousland felt 'justified in saying that the new school is influenced by the Russian cinema'.[14] The Soviet film devices of monumental and de-centred compositions and a bare, heroic Realism, had seeped into still photography in Germany.

In the summer of 1928 there was a rush of new films from Russia to Germany, and this was the very moment that Auden first arrived in Berlin, staying until Christmas that year. These films had a decisive impact on Isherwood and the Spender brothers too, when they arrived later in Berlin. Stephen based his poem *The Express* on the effect of seeing the film *Turksib* and he would later use the Soviet cinema as a yardstick in evaluating Hoyningen-Huene's photographs; comparing them with 'stills from the best Russian film'.[15] For Humphrey Spender, the Mikhail Kauffmann film *Spring,* comprised a compendium of images which could serve as models for photographs. Soviet films, seen in Berlin, multiplied and reinforced the new vision that was emerging in photography.

German and Soviet films found important London channels through the Film Society, which had been established in 1925, at the New Gallery, and, at the Avenue Pavilion cinema. Notables such as H. G. Wells, Julian Huxley, T. S. Eliot and J. B. S. Haldane were members of the Film Society as well as photographers and painters like Barbara Ker-Seymer and Edward Burra. Lang's film *Metropolis* was a direct influence on the portrait photographer, Paul Tanqueray, when it was shown in London in 1927. Some time after the screening, Tanqueray posed Anton Dolin for a photograph on a stepped dais taken from the decor of the film.[16]

But the German films which had most effect on British photographers seem to have been the analogues of the New Objectivity style: the cross-section, factual (sachlich) films and, chiefly, Ruttman's *Berlin: Die Symphonie eines Grosstadt (Berlin: The Symphony of a Great City)* (1928) which was premiered at the Film Society in January 1929. The iconography of *Berlin: The Symphony of a Great City* was influential; Ruttman's opening shots of the locomotive on the railway into the city, fragmentary in themselves, seem to have been transcribed by the British amateur film-maker and photographer, John Ahearn, in his photograph *Buffers.*[17]

Berlin: The Symphony of a Great City was filmed candidly by hidden cameras and counted among its makers the photographer, Umbo, who was about to join the new photo-journalist agency, Dephot along with Felix Man. *Berlin: The Symphony of a Great City* was film evidence, for the British, of the new documentary sensibility that was to be found in German photo-journalism, and Humphrey Spender, who was also later to work for the *Daily Mirror* and *Picture*

Post was impressed by the film. Its newsreel-like display of chance human arrangments and evanescent events on one spring day in Berlin seemed to be the essence of the new German photo-journalist style. This was the opinion of Oswell Blakeston, who had spent some time in Berlin in 1930. Explaining developments in photography in the *Architectural Review*, he defined a 'German School, which draws its inspiration, from the film newsreel; it seeks to catch • the impermanent, the moments which flash up and are gone'.[18]

Realist Portraiture in the New German Photography: Casparius and Lerski

Before his decision in 1933 to become a professional photographer, Humphrey Spender moved between Freiburg, Berlin, Vienna and London, gravitating more and more towards Realism. He would spend time examining stills from German and Soviet films, printed in *Close Up*, trying 'to decide which shots could be real and which posed'.[19] This led him to admire the work of Hans Casparius, studio photographer for the film director, G. W. Pabst. At the end of 1931, an unposed, candid photograph of half breeds in Canada, taken by Casparius, was published in *Close Up*, with the caption, 'Not Hollywood extras but the type of man you meet along the route of the C.P.R. (Canadian Pacific Railroad)'.[20] This kind of photograph followed the view put forward by Werner Gräff, in his photobook *Es kommt der neue Fotograf!* (1929) where he criticized Pictorialist assertions that models' heads should be picturesque, which, Gräff held, resulted in corrupt, spoiled photographs.

This puritan, Realist rhetoric also operated in the case of Helmar Lerski, whose ultra close-up pictures of faces were published in the photobook *Köpfe des Alltags* (1931). Kenneth Macpherson unprecedentedly gave over his editorial in *Close-Up* to review these portraits.[21] Again there was a link with film; Lerski had been a film cameraman, on another cross section (Querschnitt) film, B. Viertel's *Abenteuer eines Zehnmarkschein* (1928), *(The Adventures of a 10 Mark Note)*. Now, in 1931, through Macpherson's warm review, Lerski's portraits were presented to a British audience. Lerski succeeded in investing sitters from all social stratas with nobility, and his heroizing of manual labourers and washerwomen, was seen, by Curt Glaser, in his introduction to *Köpfe des Alltags*, to be a similar tactic to that found in Soviet films. Although the photographs were a triumph of exactitude in the New Objectivity style, the heads appeared as gigantic type images, 'Humanity with a capital H, transcends in sentiment and sentimentality its sole constituents . . . objectivism is gradually replaced by symbolism'.[22]

Lerski's slide from New Objectivity harshness towards humanitarianism seemed, to the British eye, to relate him to the London photographer, Howard Coster, who was then in the ascendant as a purveyor of giant photo-portraits under his trade sign, 'Photographer of Man'.[23] Lerski also appeared sympathetic to the British because there was something redolent of Julia Margaret Cameron's large faces of the 1860s about his portraits. Hoppé had foreshadowed certain aspects of Lerski, too, in his heads of working class men that had been shown in London at the Goupil Gallery in 1928.

The British Version of 'The New Man'

Here, then, was the obverse of the New Objectivity, a kind of 19th century, humanitarian Realism given an objectivist (sachlich) gloss. Gilbert Cousland, who had trained with Hoyningen-Huene in 1929 and had then gone on to study photography in Germany, idolized David Octavius Hill's mid-19th century portraits which had just been collected together and reproduced in a German book. Cousland saw D. O. Hill from a German standpoint, imbued with the

German values of 'blood warmth . . . (and) a master of expressionism'.[24]

It seems that Barbara Ker-Seymour obtained her copy of *Köpfe des Alltags* through her friendship with Kenneth Macpherson and Lerski's oiled and perspiring faces fascinated the London circle around her, which included Brian Howard and the painter, John Banting, at the beginning of 1932. Banting had already persuaded Barbara Ker-Seymer to imitate New Objectivity industrial still lifes of banal machinery when he arranged a storage battery for her to photograph. Barbara Ker-Seymer recalled: 'After Lerski, we began oiling people quite a lot and John (Banting) got people to cover their faces with egg white'.[25] It was against this background of overt imitation of, quite literally, the surface values found in German styles, that her *Portrait of Nancy Morris* (1932) was made, grafting the New Objectivity onto high society portraiture, a photograph which virtually constituted a homage to Lerski.

Some of the imperatives of the new German photography – attention to surface, skin texture and a dramatic three dimensionality – were becoming dissolved, in Ker-Seymer and Humphrey Spender's case, into an evocative image of the desired, mythical Weimar culture – a cypher for the mythology of sunbathing,[26] athletics, bare flesh and high technology. Although Lerski's portraits indicated a world of ascetic Gothic introspection, Ker-Seymer and Humphrey Spender developed Lerski's style among more sensuous lines. Humphrey Spender in his German *Portrait of Heinz* (1932)[27] (sun reflected on bare wet back) and *Stephen Spender* (1932–4)[28] (a monumental head in the wind, open to nature) seemed to be also invoking the 'new man' that Karl Nierendorf wrote of, in his preface to Blossfeldt's *Urformen der Kunst* (1929). 'A new kind of man is appearing: a creature who enjoys play, is confident in both air and water, tanned by the sun and determined to discover and open up a brighter world for himself'. It had been in pursuit of this light-filled, paganistic image that Brian Howard had written about his concern for 'getting into contact with life. The life that is pulsing out of the sun and the mountains'.[29] And Humphrey Spender found the photographic equivalent for this sentiment in Hans Casparius' stills taken during the production of the G. W. Pabst/A. Fanck film, *Die weisse Hölle von Piz Palu* (1929) *(The White Hell of Piz Palu)* which presented an elemental world of sun, snow and clouds, with light spiritualizing all things, like the light in Lerski's portraits.

Science and the New Objectivity

While one element in the photography of the New Objectivity emphasized spirituality and pathos, through methods of intense Realism, another, more positivist side of the New Objectivity, concentrated upon impassive scrutiny of material things and manufactured objects, without the romantic resonances that attended Lerski or Erfurth's photographs. When Roh and Tschichold's *Photo-Eye* was advertised by Zwemmers in London, it was presented with quasi-scientific undertones as 'An excellent aid to . . . intenser seeing'. The creed of impartial description was transmitted to Britain by, among others, Walter Nurnberg, the German New Objectivity photographer who emigrated to London in 1934. While he thought Lerski's *Köpfe des Alltags* photobook 'a great masterpiece',[30] he was also intensely impressed by Renger-Patzsch. From Renger-Patzsch's work he drew the conclusion that it was possible, in the act of photographing, 'not to superimpose one's personality, to stand back, and analyse clearly why a thing is what it is'.[31]

This drive towards a more positivist and analytical point of view was compelling, because in the New Objectivity photography it was often found in conjunction with scientific and para-scientific disciplines. In Auden's contemporary outlook there was a parallel wish for 'clinical' writing which incorporated

Humphrey Spender *Heinz c.*1934

medical and psycho-analytical concepts. In a similar way Blossfeldt's photographs supplemented botanical studies; Casparius' photographs were used at
Hirschfield's Institut für Sexualforschung in Berlin; while popularized anthro-
pology and ethnography provided the motivation for Bosshardt and Lechen-
perg's photo-journalist forays into Asia; and the comparative study of racial
types also began to attract Lerski in the early 1930s. Such contacts with science
appeared to act as guarantees for the impartial, objective character of the

photographs concerned.

This kind of conjunction also operated, independently, in Britain. Michael Spender was chosen, after his work with Leitz, to be the offical photographer to the 1933 Oxford University Expedition to the New Hebrides, and it was in this anthropological role that a link between the Spender family of photographers and the explorer Tom Harrisson was established. This was a link that would culminate in Humphrey Spender's work for Mass Observation, the British social survey organization, at the close of the 1930s.

The Industrial Image

German 'sachlich' industrial decor and machine culture was the magnet for the British painter Edward Wadsworth. 'Germany is marvellous',[32] he wrote after his visit in 1930. He was engrossed by the two-funnelled steam tugs of the big German rivers and praised them in *Unit 1:* perhaps it was not entirely coincidental that an image of one of the tugs, in a negative print by Andreas Feininger, had been one of the first illustrations in *Photo-Eye,* in 1929. At the end of the 1920s he abandoned oil paints for a more precise medium, tempera, which lent his paintings a hyper-Realist, New Objectivity finish. Wadsworth's pictures were owned by photographers in London,[33] and in 1929 his still lifes of manufactured objects and industrial instruments, 'modern still lifes', were counterfeited, in photographic form, by Maurice Beck and Helen McGregor, the results being published in the photomagazine *The Graphic.*[34] The images were prime objects of New Objectivity industrial photography in Britain, and, in fact, from 1925 Beck and McGregor had taken the lead in photographic advertisements for industry.[35] Around 1931 Maurice Beck was appointed as Shell-Mex's and BP's official photographer, for, by this time British industrial patrons were assimilating New Objectivity photography into their publicity, recreating the situation that had occurred in Germany a few years before, when even Hugo Erfurth, the portraitist, had undertaken 'still life' advertising work for Osram,[36] while Renger-Patzsch, Finsler and Burchartz regularly worked in advertising photography.

The Expansion of Advertising Photography

So far we have been concerned with individual contacts with German photography among vanguard groups working, for the most part, outside commercial advertising photography. Yet the New Objectivity in Britain was also fostered and anglicized in a milieu that was commercial; circulating, channelling and disseminating the new German photography under commercial pressure, on a different terrain to the initiatives and experiments of, say, Ker-Seymer.

Moreover, as British industry decayed at the end of the 1920s (while German exports doubled between 1924 and 1929, and industrial investment ran at a high 12 per cent a year),[37] advertising agencies sought out new approaches for the presentation of goods. Archaic styles of advertising were blamed as 'partly the reason why the outside world is placing Britain among the also rans',[38] and the new German photography, it was felt, might infuse energy and efficiency. In 1930 Paul Nash and Edward Burra looked to the new German photography to administer a similar rejuvenation to British art, through the means of photomontage techniques. It was in this mood that the Vice-President of the Advertising Association, C. Harold Vernon wrote in 1929; 'we English still have a knack of taking cuttings from foreign plants and growing our flowers therefrom . . . there are many who have deep-rooted prejudices against this forward movement as a whole . . . they are the sound businessmen whose enterprise and verve have contributed so much to the present flourishing condition of British industries and who can, of course, afford to sneer at the revolutionary Germans . . .'.[39]

Vernon could, in fact, afford to be ironic at the expense of laggard industrialists: the advertising industry was booming and optimistic despite the contracting economy. The biggest sector of growth was in photo-advertising; as a writer in *Photography Today* observed in 1932 – 'five years ago one could count the number of advertising studios on one hand. Today every commercial studio of note seems to carry a photographic "branch out".'[40] This growth was to be a vital precondition in the reception of the new German photography, transplanted into the British context. When Walter Nurnberg arrived in London from Berlin in 1934, with a fully formed New Objectivity style, he found a situation he described later as 'a gold rush ... Industry and commerce, offering better remuneration than the portrait client, exerted a great attraction and promoted a general stampede, as many tried to gate-crash into a newly opened market'.[41] It was symptomatic of the shift among photographers away from portraiture – which, after all, had been their principal activity – to industry, that Barbara Ker-Seymer, for example, abandoned her experimental photography of friends and society figures and entered advertising photography in the mid 1930s.

Sir William Crawford, Crawfords Reklame Agentur and the Commercial Link to Berlin

A number of factors had converged; the rise of the advertising industry in Britain; the related expansion in commercial photographic studios; the entry of continental personskrel after 1933 – Germans like Walter Nurnberg, Hungarians like Robert Lorand; the dissemination of the new German photography through photobooks and exhibitions: and, crucially, the support of key, influential figures like Sir William Crawford. Innovative stylistic models drawn from Renger-Patzsch, Max Burchartz and Hans Finsler could be adapted to an English context because, as Crawford saw it, modernism and commerce had identical interests.[42] He was a strategic figure in his role as the chairman of the leading London advertising agency, Crawfords. In July 1929 he opened the pioneering exhibition of advertising photographs at the Camera Club and, in an address, commended a study of cinema technique and emulation of the new German photography, which, with other continental sources, 'was a challenge to British works'.[43] When Walter Nurnberg showed him examples of New Objectivity photographs on a visit to London in 1933 Crawford was already very familiar with the style, which by then had secured a strong base in Britain.

Sir William Crawford was in such a particularly strategic position because his firm owned a publicity outlet in Berlin, Crawfords Reklame Agentur, which had a high reputation in Germany. In its office through the last years of the 1920s, was another key figure in Crawford's mediation of the New Objectivity in graphic design and typography as well as photography; Ashley Havinden. His brother, John Havinden, was to become the leading British commercial photographer, drawing upon the work of Moholy-Nagy and Renger-Patzsch in the early 1930s.

This international, Anglo-German, character of Crawfords' operations was important for the designer Edward McKnight-Kauffer. It is likely that it was through advertising commissions from Crawfords that he came into contact with the photography of Herbert Bayer,[44] who was a good friend of Ashley Havinden. McKnight-Kauffer used Bayer's photographs of geometrical solids as a point of departure for his own photos; he also developed the typo-photography of Tschichold,[45] and used German schemas for photomontages he constructed. In 1929 he assembled photographs of saxophonists, dancers, racing cars, riflemen and Lucia Moholy's photos of the Bauhaus into a photomontage called *1999*. This was reproduced in the leading German magazine *Gebrauchsgraphik*[46] and seemed to offer another summary of British perceptions of modern German culture, but in the style of Heartfield's composite photographs. Later in the same year Heartfield was introduced to Britain as one of the innovators pressing the new German photography into use in advertising.[47]

In 1929 the International Advertising Agency – fundamentally an Anglo-American organization – marked the beginning of German membership of its body by a Convention held in Berlin that August. In the period after the stabilization of the Mark in 1924, until the onset of the slump in 1930, Germany had been re-incorporated into the Western financial system, and the August 1929 Convention was perceived as more evidence of the German international-ist outlook. Large shows of advertising material, including New Objectivity photography, were exhibited in Berlin diffusing the style to influential individu-als – such as visiting art directors and commercial photographers. Sir William Crawford was President of the International Contact Committee and William Gaunt, joint editor of the London magazine, *Commercial Art*, spoke to the Convention. He praised the new commercial structure that was communicating and disseminating style; 'It is a wonderful thing that the outstanding successes of advertising art should be transmitted from one world capital to another . . . helping to unify the world'.[48] Gaunt's euphoria led him that autumn to write the central text which placed modern Germany squarely in the contemporary British imagination: *A Modern Utopia?; Berlin — The New Germany — The New Movement.*[49]

Salomon and Hoppé;
Exemplars of International Anglo-German Photography

The international commercial framework described by Gaunt at the Berlin Convention, acted as a support system for photography. It enabled photo-graphers like Erich Salomon to work in Britain and also brought E. O. Hoppé, the most distinguished, established British photographer into contact with Germany, while other Germans like Paul Woolf did publicity work for British Companies such as Dunlop.[50]

Erich Salomon's photography for the British magazine *The Graphic,* from around 1928, was vital for the development of photo-reportage. Indeed, the phrase 'Candid Camera' was invented for him by *The Graphic*. Many of the intimate pictures of political, financial and judicial elites that are found in his book *Berühmte Zeitgenossen* (1931) first appeared in the pages of *The Graphic*. Humphrey Spender pored over Salomon's photographs of dark conference salon discussions between European political leaders, and, when he came to photograph domino players in a pub in Bolton in 1937, he used Salomon's technique and style; while crucially inverting Salomon's social range for inclu-sion in candid portraiture.

Just as Salomon's reputation was high in Britain, Hoppé was equally known and admired in Germany. The radical leftist critic, Peter Panter, praised Hoppé in the *Deutsche Lichtbild* annual in 1930 for his purity and acuteness: 'How brightly he does it, how penetrating, how his eye pierces the world. That is the great man.' UFA, the film conglomerate and Ullstein, the giant publishing house, vied for his services. In 1929 he worked in Germany on advertising photographs for prestige luggage and travelling clothes – he had, in fact, been an advocate of commercial 'still life' advertisement photography since the the time of the Wembley exhibition in 1924. He pictured German industry in an extra-ordinary photobook for Ullstein, *Deutsche Arbeit*, which was published in 1930. In these photographs of steel works, oil tanks and electric pylons, he mixed his engrained predilections for Pictorialist symbolism with definite attempts at the New Objectivity, which is to say that he appears to have made efforts to renovate his style in the light of the prevailing new German photography.

Commodity Realism

Commercial support then, from bodies like Ullstein, Dunlop or Shell-Mex sometimes carried with it the necessity for change and adaptation to new modes of representation. This thrust was acknowledged by a writer in *Photography Today* in 1931; . . . 'the decidedly new trend in photographic vision . . . in its turn is aroused by the demands for greater reader attractiveness on the part of the advertisers ever on the search for something new and compelling'.[51]

Photo-Eye was reviewed in *Commercial Art* under the heading, 'What the Camera can do for you, the New Photography enters the field'[52] – with the clear intention that advertisers were being offered the New Objectivity as an instrument for selling. Thus, when the Berlin School of Photography, Schule Reimann – which had employed Werner Gräff – moved to London in the mid 1930s its reputation as a commercially oriented institution ensured its positive reception by leading figures in public relations and the advertising industry like Frank Pick and Jack Beddington.

The admission that commercial stimuli were determining a new style in photography, which emphasized manufactured textures and high finishes on products – a style of Commodity Realism – was made by F. J. Mortimer in 1932, when he accepted that, 'the remunerative side of the work had not been the least of the incentives for doing it'.[53] The advantages of such photographic Commodity Realism over manual, drawn representations had been earlier emphasized by Carl Georg Heise in his preface to Renger-Patzsch's photobook, *Die Welt ist schön*: and by *The Times* in its review of the exhibition of advertising photographs that Sir William Crawford had opened in July 1929; 'Photography is strong exactly where painting and drawing weak, that is to say in the precise reproduction of objects, particularly as regards surface qualities'.[54]

It was upon this that Walter Nurnberg proposed to concentrate. While he was still a student at the Berlin Schule Reimann around 1932, he set himself the formidable task of photographing, over a nine month period, representative items of household goods, kitchen utensils and tools that it was possible to hire from the Berlin trades directory, in the New Objectivity style of Renger-Patzsch. Here was a Herculean task by a photographer, in training for a commercial career to be sought in Britain, making exact accounts of the surface and textures of homely, banal objects like cast-iron frying pans and egg slicers.

Whereas Pictorialism had presented the photographer in the role of painter and elevated aesthete, the new German photography produced an opposite image of the photographer well-integrated with everyday life. This was the role Oswell Blakeston announced in an article in 1931, *Selling Machinery through Photography,* which introduced Moholy-Nagy, Aenne Biermann and Rudolf Kramer's industrial photography to the pages of *Commercial Art.* Implicitly attacking Pictorialism, he wrote: 'Art is working back into life, to what we see and know . . . The day of photographs bearing no relation to life, which have to be left in untrodden galleries, is over.'[55]

Channels of Diffusion; The Impact of the Photobook and Magazine

The most influential way in which the new German photography passed into the British visual imagination was through the spread of reproductions, in the original photobooks and in photographic and advertising magazines, between 1929 until 1932.

Blossfeldt's *Urformen der Kunst,* published by Zwemmers as *Art Forms in Nature* in 1929, was given enormous publicity in *The Times* (a surprising but consistent ally of the new photography) through the intervention of its art editor U. V. Bogaerde. Besides publishing reproductions, *The Times* also devoted a leading article – not a review – to endorse Blossfeldt, and the leader drew comfort from the pantheistic views expressed in Karl Nierendorf's introduction which reconciled man, technical developments and Nature.[56] The ex-Vorticist, turned architect, Frederick Etchells reviewed *Art Forms in Nature* for the *Architectural Review*,[57] the magazine which also carried the first British reproductions from Walter Hege's photographs of the Parthenon. Hege's picture[58] was, significantly, captioned 'At Close Range', again mobilizing the rhetoric of the close-up within the new photography.

The celebrated image of flat irons from Renger-Patzsch's *Die Welt ist schön* was featured very early on, in 1929, in *Commercial Art*, a magazine staffed by Germanophiles like William Gaunt with contributing writers such as John Harrisson, a designer and a keen collector of German art, who repeatedly advocated a 'new simplicity'.[59] An Otto Dix-type photo-portrait of a fat lady by Hugo Erfurth scandalized readers of *Photography Today* in 1932; in its 'sachlich' grotesqueness it was 'a subject that would appal most photographers'.[60] Thus by 1932, photographs by the leading Germans – Biermann, Burchartz, Renger-Patzsch, Erfurth, Hege, Finsler, Henri,-Lerski, and Salomon had all appeared in English publications.

Der Querschnitt

'We were passionately interested in everything German – the films and the photobooks. We also had *Querschnitt*, and, even though we couldn't read German, this really was no problem'.[61] Barbara Ker-Seymer's testimony to the popularity, in certain vanguard circles, of the German prototype for Stefan Lorant's *Lilliput*, indicates another source for the insurgent new photography. In January 1931 the magazine had a special issue cross-sectioning 'England and the English'. British photographers, artists and writers who obtained this copy saw England mirrored according to the drives of the new photography – in mixes of documentary photographs, juxtaposed images and close-ups. It was through *Querschnitt* that Humphrey Spender discovered Munkacsi, whose high-level view, from 1931, onto a German street, empty except for a policeman, called *Der kategorische Imperativ*, lingered on in Spender's imagination throughout the 1930s.

George Grosz had been an occasional contributor to *Querschnitt* and Brian Howard found his graphic style irritatingly dominant in William Gaunt's attempt at an urban cross-section book *London Promenade* (1930). The fact that Howard could call his review of Gaunt's book,[62] 'Anglo-German Art' only underlined the influence which was now being exerted from contemporary German culture. It was at this moment that Grosz's drawings were published in a paperback edition in London[63] and, in June 1934, he was given a one-man exhibition at the Mayor Gallery.

Burra and Nash:
the Painter as convert to Photomontage and the New Objectivity

In 1930 the influence of the new German photography began to be marked upon some vanguard artists who had not travelled to Berlin but had been exposed to the photobooks instead.

Grosz's most adept follower in British painting, Edward Burra, became a major collector of the German photobooks, purchasing the Fototek books, *Photo-Eye*, and others from Zwemmers during 1930. This was the year that Burra and Paul Nash began to implement photomontage procedures in joint collaborative pictures, such as *Rough on Rats*,[64] based on works illustrated in Burra's copy of *Moholy-Nagy Fototek 1:* (1930). In June 1930 Burra wrote to Barbara Ker-Seymer that 'we never bother to paint in this part now, we just stick things on instead'.[65] Burra's predilection for the bizarre as a genre was probably encouraged by Roh's statement in *Photo-Eye* which challenged Carl Georg Heise's thesis that the world as revealed in the new photography of Renger-Patzsch, was beautiful. Roh wrote ' . . . the world is also exciting, cruel and weird'.[66]

Burra was familiar, too, with Germaine Krull's photographs, to the extent that, while in the south of France in 1931 he copied her techniques and took photographs 'by the Germaine Krull method' – as he wrote to Barbara Ker-

Albert Renger-Patzsch *Breakwater*

Seymer.[67] Her photobook *100 x Paris* (1929) with its mixture of steep high level views and informal street shots also deeply impressed Humphrey Spender.

With this extensive knowledge of the new German photography it seems possible that Burra, given his close collaboration at this stage with Paul Nash, may have introduced the latter to Renger-Patzsch's *Die Welt ist schön*. For the book must be counted as a major determinant on Paul Nash's own photographs around 1932. Possibly Renger-Patzsch's nature photographs of tree trunks, ponds and gardens and woodpiles were cues for Nash. His photographs, c. 1932, of breakwaters[68] can be closely compared with Renger-Patzsch's photograph in *Die Welt ist schön* dealing with the same subject. Nash's relationship to Neue Sachlichkeit photography was suspected a few years later: in 1938 Andor Kraszna-Krausz, a publisher of German photobooks and *Close-up*'s one-time Berlin correspondent, had emigrated to London. Here he was shown Paul Nash's photographs by Oswell Blakeston, and Kraszna-Krausz, who knew Renger-Patzsch's work in some detail, pronounced Nash's images to be nothing other than New Objectivity in style and content.[69]

Similarly no examination of Nash's *Atlantic Voyage* photographs of 1931[70] can afford to neglect specific photographic models from the New Objectivity corpus with which Nash was familiar, like the ship funnel photograph by the German, Stankowski, that was reproduced in the *Photographie* 1930 annual which Nash owned[71]; Finsler's *Ship's funnel* 1929 is yet another possible model: in the *Atlantic* photographs Nash had chosen a favourite icon of the Purists and Constructivists – the liner; and deployed a classic New Objectivity point of view on fragments of ship architecture and machinery.

Oswell Blakeston may also have been the mediator to Paul Nash of Florence Henri's still life photographs. She had trained at the Bauhaus and Blakeston had met her in Paris and written about her pictures for *Advertising Display* in 1931. Her still lifes from 1928 often used domestic items like cotton reels and small balls with mirrors – their New Objectivity Constructivism qualified by an edge of Surrealist speculation about reflections and objects. This may have appealed to

Hans Finsler *Ship's funnels* 1929

Nash, for his still life photographs around 1934 also manipulated the same vocabulary of forms,[72] as did his paintings, especially *Landscape from a Dream* (1936) in the early and middle 1930s. Nash could also have seen Henri's work reproduced in the Paris Constructivist magazine *Cercle et Carré* or at her exhibition in Paris in 1930; she was, surprisingly, also represented at The Royal Photographic Society exhibitions in 1932 and 1934. The New Objectivity and photomontage, then, played an important part in the photographs and paintings of Edward Burra and Paul Nash at the beginning of the 1930s: yet, apart from conventional citations of Moholy-Nagy's influence on Nash, the impact of German photography has been ignored within British art history dealing with this period.

The Breakthrough of Exhibitions of the New German Photography in London 1929–1932

We have already traced several interacting channels that were distributing the new German photography to Britain – the media of film, photobooks and magazine reproductions; institutions like cinemas or advertising agencies and, of course, the personal networks of family and friends. Actual exhibitions of German photography were few in number, but important in their effect of precipitating discussion and controversy. In October 1929 Zwemmers mounted a show of Blossfeldt's photographs, organized by Robert Wellington to complement the publication of *Art Forms in Nature*. But the moment of breakthrough may be assigned to the exhibition of *German Advertising Photographs* at the Camera Club in February 1930. The Camera Club had been the location of vanguardist dissension in the Pictorialist period, around 1910. Now, at the beginning of the 1930s, it was revivified, showing New Objectivity work by Finsler and Sasha Stone. 'We have heard many eulogistic remarks about the so-called German style of photography' wrote George Mewes in *Photography*[73] afterwards, yet the inclusion of photographs like Finsler's *(Osram) Lightbulb* (which had been reproduced in *Photo-Eye*[74]) seemed eccentric to the defenders of the staid state of Pictoralist photography. *The British Journal of Photography* was frankly hostile, disbelieving the Germans had any status at all as leading photographers and complaining of the 'excessively hard gradations'[75] to be found in the pictures. This last, of course, could not help but be offensive to eyes steeped in Pictorialist haze and fine tonalities. Close-ups enraged the same critic . . . 'composition is summed up in the favourite German word "kolossal". The method is to select some bit of the article . . . and to enlarge it to a degree which results in ugliness'.[76] But *The Times* applauded 'possibilities of creating interest by the unexpected relation of objects and jumps in scale'.[77]

The resistance and conservatism reflected in *The British Journal of Photography's* criticisms were being eroded by a coalition of interests – the taste of the commercial photographers, for example, which was being changed by increased coverage of the German photography in advertising magazines and the new international annuals like *Photographie*. The taste of the vanguard photographers, too, as we have seen, was aligned towards Germany; the euphoric internationalist ideology of Germany as a utopia and the destination for liberal industrial societies was also widespread. The enlightened criticism of Gilbert Cousland, newly returned from work with Hoyningen-Huene and study in Germany, represented an insurgent voice within *The British Journal of Photography*. He presented The Royal Photographic Society with a copy of Gräff's *Es kommt der neue Fotograf!* and praised the severe works of Finsler, Moholy-Nagy, Burchartz and Renger-Patzsch as, 'in a class by themselves'[78] as they appeared in *Photographie* in 1930. He then wondered 'if the Purist movement will be forthcoming at the Royal and Salon exhibitions'.[79] Oswell Blakeston was pessimistic on this point – 'those who go into the London Salon must believe that photography is at a dead end'[80] and then went on to contrast the Salon's fossilized Pictorialism with the work of 'really creative photographers'[81] like Lerski.

The arguments for the new photography were promoted by the publication in September 1931 of the British version of the continental annuals *Photographie* and *Deutsche Lichtbild*; the Studio's *Modern Photography*. This presented the new photography by such tactics as juxtaposing manufactured and natural objects – a Maurice Beck photo of a crank-shaft with Paul Woolf's photo of a plant, for example[82] – an aesthetic form that both Heise and Nierendorf had proposed in their writings. *The British Journal of Photography* capitulated; 'It is emphatically one (book) which photographers, and especially commercial photographers, must have if they are to keep in touch with the kinds of photography which are pushing their way into public notice'.[83] F. J. Mortimer had written off the new photography as an ephemeral, extremist tendency in his introduction to *Photograms of the Year* in 1931; but the following year he grudgingly changed his opinion, conceding the prevalance of cinematic inspiration, Commodity Realism and close-ups.

The permeation continued: in 1932 there were two events that signalled the passage of the values and styles of new German photography into British culture. A certain threshold of acceptance had been reached; in February the Publicity Club of London and The Royal Photographic Society held a joint meeting to discuss photography in advertising[84] where the majority of speakers acknowledged the pre-eminence of a new style, composed of clarity, simplicity, the Soviet film, and open, natural lighting.[85]

Another definite turning point in sanctioning the new German photography was an exhibition, *Works by Twenty-Seven Photographers,* held at the Wertheim Gallery in London in August 1932. The Wertheim acted as a pilot institution for the New Objectivity in London by showing German photographs in a West End Art Gallery rather than at the Camera Club. It had shown John Banting's paintings in 1929, at a time when his portraits could only be classified as New Objectivity, since they were very close in style to the German Neue Sachlichkeit painters Grethe Jurgens, Schrimpf and Greta Overbeck Schenk. Alfred Flechtheim, the Berlin owner of *Der Querschnitt* and patron of the New Objectivity had included Banting in his *Omnibus* magazine in 1931, further confirming links with Germany.

The 1932 Wertheim photography exhibition was organized by a London advertising agency art director, R. Haughton James. International in scope, it was a major exhibition with Renger-Patzsch, Herbert Bayer and Moholy-Nagy exhibiting alongside the emerging young British New Objectivity photographer, John Havinden. This confident and large scale display marked a change in the cultural climate. Franz Roh must have gauged this change, for there is evidence that around 1932 he visited London, calling on leading photographers, including Ker-Seymer, discussing their work and the feasibility of a photobook reproducing their photographs.[86]

Conclusion: London–Berlin–London

John Havinden was, in fact, construed by some contemporaries to be a photographer following Renger-Patzsch's project as it had been sketched by Carl George Heise. G. H. Saxon Mills described Havinden selecting a banal, unnoticed railway signal and photographing it to 'make it seem . . . the thing of dramatic beauty, which it is. Such photography . . . lifts the scales from our eyes for a moment to the wonders of the world'.[87] *The Times* critic testified to another tenet of Patzsch-ian New Objectivity at the Wertheim show; 'where photography scores is in bringing out the thinginess of things'.[88] Noel Griggs' picture of *Battersea Power Station* (1933),[89] seemed linked to Erich Mendelsohn's photographic versions of towering American buildings and factories, that had been gathered in his *Bilderbuch eines Architekten* (1925) – a hybrid of Expressionism and New Objectivity. In all, a number of British photographers, had now comprehended the aims and directions of the new German movement: Gilbert Cousland, Humphrey Spender, Douglas Glass, Edith Tudor-Hart, Peggy Delius, Shaw Wildman, John Havinden and Noel Griggs, had all, by 1932, incorporated German styles.

But the overwhelming cultural event which would shape the course of German and British photography in the middle and late 1930s, falls beyond the historical limits of this survey. The emigration of leading German photographers, photographic publishers and picture editors from Nazi rule began in 1933; this brought a pool of talent to London, which reinforced the incorporation of the new German photography into the mainstream of British culture. These included: Lucia Moholy; Laszlo Moholy-Nagy; Grete Stern; Felix Man; Hans Casparius; Walter Nurnberg; Stefan Lorant; Andor Kraszna-Krausz; Kurt Hubschmann; Alex Strasser and Simon Guttmann. We have only glanced at the roles of three of these individuals: Andor Kraszna-Krausz, Hans Casparius and Walter Nurnberg, but Kraszna-Krausz summed up the background to his own departure from Germany in this way:

Around 1936 it became clear to me that the Nazis were not going to be checked by the French or British and that war was inevitable – why should I die on the wrong side? I had a choice – to go to England or America, but I preferred England. So I started commuting between Germany and England for a time looking for a job; because the psychological pressure became very bad, you can't live in an environment you disagree with 100% ; you can't live at all, if, every morning, even before you opened the paper you would disagree with every headline. The impact was devastating . . . and, in the Hitler years, no-one would use the term "New Objectivity", because it was identified with the Weimar Republic.[90]

1. Cf. illustration to M. J. Lancaster *Portrait of a Failure*, Anthony Blond, 1968.
2. This view was put forward by Stephen Spender in *The Thirties*, A Symposium at the University of Sussex, 9 February 1972.
3. Correlli Barnet *The Collapse of British Power*, Eyre Methuen, 1972, pp.320 and 322.
4. Jimmy Stern quoted in M. J. Lancaster op.cit. p.258.
5. Stephen Spender (Review) African Mirage, *New Statesman*, 7 May 1935, p.800.
6. Ibid.
7. Interview with the author, June 1978.
8. *Close-Up*, October 1929, p.322.
9. Advertisement in *Close Up*, early 1930.
10. Introduction, *Modern Photography*, 1933–4, p.12.
11. *Photograms of the Year*, 1932, p.3.
12. A. Kraszna-Krausz; interview with the author, June 1978.
13. *Posters and Publicity Yearbook*, 1929, p.13.
14. *British Journal of Photography*, 15 August, 1930. p.496.
15. Spender op.cit.
16. Paul Tanqueray, information to the author, June 1978.
17. Reproduced *Modern Photography*, 1932, p.42.
18. Oswell Blakeston 'The Still Camera Today'.*Architectural Review*, April 1932, pp.154–7. Blakeston's definition would fall into the last of the following three categories by which A. Kraszna-Krausz usefully divides the new German photography of the period.
   '(1) The New Objectivity proper of Renger-Patzsch – an objective functional approach thinking about things and recording them; an approach which was very closely married to clean cut, superior craftsmanship.
   (2) A stream represented by the Bauhaus . . . a much more dilettante approach, in the sense of cutting loose from all existing technology, and in Moholy-Nagy's case turning the accidental element into a virtue . . .
   (3) The third stream was the new picture journalists, started more by Salomon than anyone else, and the inspiration was the new cameras . . . Hutton and Man came from that stream.'
   Interview with the author June 1978. In Britain it was the first and third of these categories that were well received and became primarily identified with the new German photography.
19. Interview with the author, July 1978.
20. *Close-Up*, December 1931, p.274.
21. As Is, *Close-Up*, September 1931, pp.220–4.
22. Ibid.
23. See *Commercial Art*, June 1932, pp.242–5, for Howard Coster's work.

24. Gilbert Cousland, 'Expressionism in Publicity Photography', *Penrose Annual*, 1934, p.86.
25. Interview with the author, July 1977.
26. For a contemporary British account of the German cult of sunbathing see Cicely Hamilton 'Sunbathing', *Weekend Review*, 6 May 1933, p.524.
27. Reproduced *Photography Yearbook*, 1935, p.191.
28. Reproduced *Photography Yearbook*, 1935, p.193.
29. M. J. Lancaster, op. cit., p.244.
30. Interview with the author, June 1978.
31. Interview with the author, June 1978.
32. Letter to Maxwell Armfield, 1936, Tate Gallery Archive.
33. Mrs Bertram Park owned Wadsworth's *Shells*, 1927, for example.
34. *The Graphic*, 30 August, 1929, p.35.
35. See, for example, their work for Lyons, reproduced in *Penrose Annual*, 1926.
36. See *Gebrauchsgraphik*, **6**, 1929, no.6, p.60.
37. Correlli Barnet, op. cit., p.334.
38. *Commercial Art*, April 1930, pp.37–8.
39. C. Harold Vernon, 'A Review of Press Advertising', *Posters and Publicity*, 1929, p.87.
40. *Photography Today*, 5 March 1932, p.254.
41. Walter Nurnberg 'Advertising Photography', *Photography as a Career*, Focal Press, 1944, p.71.
42. See, for example, his Preface to *Modern Publicity*, 1930.
43. Reported in *The British Journal of Photography*, 19 July 1929, p.426.
44. Compare McKnight Kauffer's photograph reproduced *Commercial Art*, March 1931, p.154 with Bayer's late 1920s photographs of cones and cubes.
45. Compare Tschichold's space frames with McKnight Kauffer's *Charing Cross Exhibition Scheme 2*, Victoria and Albert Museum.
46. *Gebrauchsgraphik*, **6**, no.5, 1929, p.45.
47. Errell 'Photography in Advertising', *Posters and Publicity Yearbook*, 1929, p.13.
48. His address is published in *Commercial Art*, October 1929, p.144.
49. *The Studio*, December 1929, pp.859–865.
50. See *Commercial Art*, December 1933, p.234.
51. *Photography Today*, 20 November 1934, p.87.
52. *Commercial Art*, May 1930, pp.257–66.
53. *Photograms of Year 1932*, p.3.
54. *The Times*, 5 October 1929, p.13.
55. *Commercial Art*, August 1931, pp.67–9.
56. *The Times*, 5 October 1929, p.13.
57. *Architectural Review*, December 1929, p.300.
58. *Architectural Review*, July 1932, pl.VI.
59. See John Harrisson's articles for *Commercial Art*, June 1930, 257–266, and December 1930, pp.276–280. He was one of the organizers of the large *Twentieth Century German Art Exhibition* at the Burlington Galleries in July 1938.
60. *Photography Today*, 5 April 1932, p.9.
61. Barbara Ker-Seymer in an interview with the author, June 1977.
62. 'Anglo-German Art', *Architectural Review*, November 1930, p.219.
63. *A Post-War Museum*, Faber and Faber, May 1931.
64. No.26, Edward Burra Exhibition, Tate Gallery, 1973.
65. John Rothenstein, *Edward Burra*, Tate Gallery, 1973, p.88.
66. Franz Roh, 'Mechanism and Expression', *Photo-Eye*, 1929, p.16.
67. Letter from Edward Burra to Barbara Ker-Seymer, 27 September 1931.
68. See especially Andrew Causey, *Paul Nash's Photographs, Document and Image*, Tate Gallery, 1973, pl.7.
69. Information from Andor Kraszna-Krausz, June 1978.
70. See Causey, op. cit. pls. 3 and 5.
71. Paul Nash, 'Art and Photography', *The Listener*, VI, 1931, pp.868–9.
72. Compare Henri's *Komposition Zwirnwollen* or *Abstract Composition* 1928, reproduced in *Florence Henri*, Martano Editore, Torino, with Nash's *Poised Objects*, pl.27, *Still Life on a Car Roof*, pl.28, or *Still Life*, pl.31 in Causey, op. cit.
73. *Photography*, August 1932, p.32.
74. *Photo-Eye*, 14.
75. *The British Journal of Photography*, 15 August 1930, p.496.
76. Ibid.
77. *The Times*, 26 February 1930, p.12.
78. *The British Journal of Photography*, 15 August 1930, p.496.
79. Ibid.
80. *Close-Up*, December 1932, p.299.
81. Ibid.
82. *Modern Photography*, 1931, pp.18–19.
83. *The British Journal of Photography*, 11 September 1931, p.548.
84. This is reported in *Photography Today*, 20 February 1932, p.224.
85. Cf Howard Wadman's recollections of this important meeting in *Photography*, August 1934, p.6.
86. Information from Barbara Ker-Seymer, August 1978.
87. *Commercial Art*, July 1931, p.7.
88. *The Times*, 2 August 1932, p.8.
89. Shown at the Professional Photographers Association Exhibition 1933, reproduced *Photography*, October 1933.
90. Interview with the author, June 1978.

Acknowledgements

The publishers would like to thank the following for permission to include copyright material:

9   Preface to A. Renger-Patzsch *Die Welt ist schön* Munich, Kurt Wolff Verlag 1928. English translation © *Camera* magazine, Switzerland 1978
15 *Photographie und Kunst* by A. Renger-Patzsch first published in *Das Deutsche Lichtbild* 1929. ©Ernst Renger-Patzsch. English translation by Trevor Walmsley. ©Arts Council of Great Britain 1978.
17 Preface to Karl Blossfeldt *Urformen der Kunst* Tübingen, Verlag Ernst Wasmuth 1928. English translation by Jill Hollis, first published in *Karl Blossfeldt photographs* Museum of Modern Art, Oxford 1978
20 *Neues von Blumen* published in Walter Benjamin *Gesammelte Schriften Bd 3,* ©Suhrkamp Verlag, Frankfurt am Main 1972. All rights reserved. English translation by Jill Hollis, first published in *Karl Blossfeldt photographs* Museum of Modern Art, Oxford 1978.
23 *Photography and Modern Art* first published in *The Listener* 27 July 1932. ©Paul Nash Trust.
25 Foreword to *Es kommt der neue Fotograf!* Berlin, Hermann Reckendorf Verlag 1929. ©Ursula Graeff-Hirsch. English translation by P. S. Falla. ©Arts Council of Great Britain 1978.
29 *Mechanism and expression* Introduction to Franz Roh and Jan Tschichold *Foto-Auge Oeil et Photo Photo-Eye* Tübingen, Ernst Wasmuth Verlag 1929. ©Dr Juliane Roh.
35 *Exhibition in Stuttgart, June 1929, and its Effects* first published in *Close Up* 29 December 1929. ©A. Kraszna-Krausz.
37 Review first published in *Close Up* February 1930. ©Oswell Blakeston.
39 *The literary dispute about photography* Introduction to Franz Roh *Aenne Biermann: Fototek 2* Berlin, Klinkhardt and Biermann 1930. ©Dr Juliane Roh.
43 *Recapitulation* first published in *Close Up* March 1931. ©Oswell Blakeston.
45 *Her vor die Kamera!* first published in *Das Neue Bild c.*1930. English translation by P. S. Falla. ©Arts Council of Great Britain 1978.
47 *Das Auge des Arbeiters* first published in *Der Arbeiter-Fotograf* V, H.7, S.151, 1930. English translation by P. S. Falla. ©Arts Council of Great Britain.
51 *Aufgaben und Ziele* first published in *Der Arbeiter-Fotograf* V, H.5, S.100, 1931. English translation by P. S. Falla. ©Arts Council of Great Britain 1978.
55 Introduction to August Sander *Antlitz der Zeit* Munich, Kurt Wolff/Transmare Verlag 1929. English translation by Marion Schneider, first published in *People of the 20th Century. Photographs of August Sander* ©Scottish Photography Group, Edinburgh, 1977. Acknowledgement to Erbengemeinschaft Döblin, Nice, and Walter-Verlag, Olten.
61 Introduction fo Helmar Lerski *Köpfe des Alltags* Berlin, Hermann Reckendorf Verlag 1931. English translation by P. S. Falla. ©Arts Council of Great Britain 1978.
65 *As Is* first published in *Close Up* 19 September 1931. ©Kenneth Macpherson.
69 *Kleine Geschichte der Photographie* first published in *Die Literarische Welt* 18 September, 25 September and 20 October 1931. All rights reserved ©Suhrkamp Verlag, Frankfurt am Main. English translation by Kingsley Shorter.
77 *Photo Eye of the 1920s* first published in *New Mexico Studies in Fine Arts* Volume II 1977. ©University of New Mexico.
87 *Urbanism and Technological Utopianism* ©Herbert Molderings 1978. A revised version of *Überlegungen zur Fotografie der Neuen Sachlichkeit und des Bauhauses* first published in *Kritische Berichte* Nos 2/3 1977.
95 *Renger-Patzsch: New Realist Photographer* ©Brian Stokoe 1978.
101 *Photography and the Neue Sachlichkeit movement* first published in *Neue Sachlichkeit and German Realism of the Twenties* Arts Council of Great Britain. ©Ute Eskildsen 1978.
113 *London–Berlin–London.* ©David Mellor 1978.

Photographs

The publishers would like to thank the following for permission to include copyright material:

2　Albert Renger-Patzsch *Die Welt ist schön* pl.76. ©Galerie Wilde, Cologne.
8　Advertisement. Courtesy of Dorothy Bohm, London.
14　Albert Renger-Patzsch *Ruhrgebiet* 1930. ©Galerie Wilde, Cologne.
18　Karl Blossfeldt *Art Forms in Nature* pl.19. ©Galerie Wilde, Cologne.
22　Cover of Karl Blossfeldt *Art Forms in Nature* A. Zwemmer, London, 1929.
26　*Bald head of Oskar Schlemmer* Werner Gräff *Es kommt der neue Fotograf!* p.52. ©T. Lux Feininger.
28　Franz Roh and Jan Tschichold *Photo Eye* pl.35. Courtesy of Galerie Klihm, Munich.
33　Franz Roh and Jan Tschichold *Photo Eye* pl.14. ©Regula Lips-Finsler.
36　Exhibition poster. Courtesy of Kunstbibliothek, Berlin.
37　Florence Henri *Composition – Cotton reels* 1928. Courtesy of Professor Dr Marlis Steinert.
38　Franz Roh *Aenne Biermann – Fototek 2* pl.60.
42　Franz Roh *Aenne Biermann – Fototek 2* pl.36.
44　*Fahnengruppe, Der Arbeiter-Fotograf* V (1931) H.11, S.283. Courtesy of Prometh Verlag, Cologne.
46　Cover of *Der Arbeiter-Fotograf* V (1931) H.9. Courtesy of Prometh Verlag, Cologne.
48　*Wir bauern eine neue Welt, Der Arbeiter-Fotograf* IV (1930) H.7, S.153. Courtesy of Prometh Verlag, Cologne.
50　*Bauern kämpfen mit uns, Der Arbeiter-Fotograf* IV (1930) H.7, S.157. Courtesy of Prometh Verlag, Cologne.
54　August Sander *Secretary, Cologne* 1931.
60　Helmar Lerski *Köpfe des Alltags* pl.78.
66　Helmar Lerski *Köpfe des Alltags* pl.50.
70　August Sander *Peasant couple, Westerwald* 1932.
73　Albert Renger-Patzsch *Die Welt ist schön* pl.68. ©Galerie Wilde, Cologne.
74　Cover of *Arbeiter Illustrierte Zeitung* 27 November 1932. Photograph ©Frau Gertrud Heartfield.
76　Hannah Höch *Geselligkeit* 1925. Courtesy of Annely Juda Fine Art, London.
82　Herbert Bayer *Small harbour, Marseilles* 1928. Courtesy of Galerie Klihm, Munich.
88　Erich Mendelsohn *Amerika* pl.73
94　Albert Renger-Patzsch *Die Welt ist schön* pl.67. ©Galerie Wilde, Cologne.
100　Cover of *Berliner Illustrirte Zeitung* 11 January 1931.
108　*Berliner Illustrirte Zeitung* 12 July 1931. Courtesy of the Wiener Library, London.
112　Erich Salomon *Berühmte Zeitgenossen in unbewachten Augenblick* Stuttgart, J. Engelhorn Nachf., 1931, pl.10. ©Estate of Erich Salomon.
114　Barbara Ker-Seymer *Portrait of Nancy Morris* 1932 ©Barbara Ker-Seymer.
119　Humphrey Spender *Heinz* 1935 *Photography Year Book* 1931, p.191. ©Humphrey Spender.
125　Albert Renger-Patzsch *Die Welt ist schön* pl.41. ©Galerie Wilde, Cologne.
126　Hans Finsler *Ship's funnel* 1929. Courtesy of Die Neue Sammlung, Staatliches Museum für angewandte Kunst, Munich. ©Regula Lips-Finsler.
132　Hugo Erfurth *Alfred Flechtheim* c.1930. Courtesy of Fotografische Sammlung im Museum Folkwang, Essen and Gottfried Erfurth.

The publishers apologise to any copyright holders that they have been unable to trace.

Index

All entries in this index refer to page numbers. Figures in bold type indicate illustrations – magazine, book and exhibition titles are given in italics.

Abdy Gallery 24
Advertising Association 120
Advertising Display 126
Ahearn, John 116
Amerika 90, 129
Antlitz der Zeit, Das 6, 55, 71, 106
Arbeiter-Fotograf, Der **46,** 47, 51, 52, 53, 92, 101, 109, 110
Arbeiter-Illustrierte-Zeitung (AIZ) **74,** 92, 109, 110, 115
Architectural Review 117, 124, 129, 130
Art Forms in Nature see *Urformen der Kunst*
Association of Worker Photographers 51, 52
ASSO Group 102
Atget, Eugène 69, 75, 83
Auden, W. H. 113, 116, 118
Author as Producer, The 7, 99, 109
Avenue Pavilion 116

Bacon, Francis 113
Banting, John 118, 128
Baudelaire, Charles 73, 75
Bauhaus 6, 7, 77, 78, 80, 84, 87, 90, 92, 103, 111, 115, 121, 126, 129
Baumeister, Willy 86
Bayer, Herbert **28, 82,** 84, 85, 90, 121, 128, 130
Beaton, Cecil 35
Beck, Maurice 120, 128
Beddington, Jack 123
Benjamin, Walter 5, 6, 7, 20, 69, 93, 95, 98, 99, 109
Berliner Illustrirte Zeitung **100,** 105, 111, 115
Berlin: Die Symphonie eines Grosstadt 116
Berlin School of Photography see Schule Reimann
Beruhmte Zeitgenossen 122
Biermann, Aenne 5, **38,** 39, **42,** 43, 92, 110, 123, 124
Bifur 60
Bigge, John 129
Bilderbuch eines Architekten see *Amerika*
Blakeston, Oswell 5, 37, 43, 115, 117, 123, 126, 127, 129
Block, Fritz 104
Blossfeldt, Karl 5, 7, 17, **18.** 19, 20, **22,** 23, 72, 91. 104, 105, 118, 123, 127
Book of New Artists 79
Born, Wolfgang 111
Bosshardt, Walter 119
Brecht, Bertholt 72
Breuer, Robert 104
Breuning, Margaret 93
British Journal of Photography 127, 129, 130
British Petroleum 120
Brockhaus, H. 39
Bruckmann, Peter 93
Bruehl, Anton 104, 108
Bruguière, Francis 35
Burchartz, Max 92, 107, 108, 120, 121, 124, 127
Burra, Edward 24, 116, 120, 124, 127, 130
Byron, Robert 24

Cabinet of Dr Caligari, The 86
Cahiers d'Art 77, 83
Camera Club 121, 127, 128
Cameron, J. M. 117
Casparius, Hans 117, 118, 129
Cavalcanti, Alberto 78
Cercle et Carré 127
Champs Délicieux 84
Chaplin, Charles 86
Chorgestühl von Cappenburg, Die 95
Circus, The 86
Citroen, Paul 77
Clair, Réné 86
Close Up 86, 115, 117, 126, 129, 130
Cocteau, Jean 113
Cologne Progressives 106
Commercial Art 123, 130
Condé Nast 81, 83
Corbusier, Le 77
Coster, Howard 117, 129
Cousland, Gilbert 116, 117, 127, 129, 130
Crawford, Sir William 121, 122, 123
Crawfords Reklame Agentur 121
Cunningham, Imogen 35, 81

Dacqué, Edgar 13
Daily Mirror 116
Dame, Die 93
Delius, Peggy 129
Delius, Rudolf von 104
Demachy, Robert 101
Dephot 26, 116
Deutsche Arbeit 122
Deutsche Lichtbild, Das 15, 96, 97, 98, 99, 102, 103, 122, 128
Deutsche Photographische Austellung 110
Deutsche Werkbund see Werkbund
Deutschland 97
Diaghilev, Serge 113
Diesel, Eugen 90
Dinge, Die 91, 195
Dix, Otto 83
Döblin, Alfred 6, 55, 71, 106
Dolin, Anton 116
Dortu, Max 6, 45
Dreyer, Carl 86
Duchamp, Marcel 79
Dunlop 122, 123
Dupont, E. A. 86
Dürer, Albrecht 12

Ecce-photo 92
Eggeling, Viking 78
Einstein, Albert 113
Eisenstaedt, Alfred 108
Eisenstein, Sergei 67, 71, 79, 86, 116
Eisen und Stahl 90
Eliot, T. S. 116
Entr'acte 86
Erfurth, Hugo 83, 110, 118, 120, 124, **132**
Ernst, Max 34, 37
Errell 110, 116, 130

Eskildsen, Ute 6, 7, 101
Es kommt der neue Fotograf! 5, 25, 85, 90, 111, 116, 117, 127
Etchells, Frederick 124
Etoile de Mer, L' 86
Etudes de nu 93
Evening Post, New York 93

Feininger, Andreas 35, 80, 120
Feininger, Lux **26,** 103
Film Society 116
Film und Foto 5, 7, 29, 35, **36,** 77, 78, 83, 85, 90, 111, 115
Finsler, Hans **33,** 35, 92, 96, 104, 120, 121, 124, **126,** 127
Flechtheim, Alfred 128, 132
Formen des Leben 91
Form, Die 77, 78, 85, 93, 104, 108, 110
foto-auge see *Photo-Eye*
Fototek Series 5, 39, 43, 124
Friedrich, C. D. 10
Friemert, Chup 105
Fuhrmann, Ernst 93
Funke, Jaromir 102

Gaunt, William 97, 98, 122, 124
Gebrauchsgraphik 107, 121, 130
German Advertising Photographs 127
Gernsheim, Helmut 98
Giedion, Sigfried 78
Glaser, Curt 6, 61, 117
Glass, Douglas 129
Goethe 71
Gorny, Hein 92
Goupil Gallery 117
Gräff, Werner 5, 7, 25, 35, 85, 86, 90, 111, 117, 123, 127
Grandville, Gérard 20
Graphic, The 120, 122, 130
Griggs, Noel 129
Gropius, Walter 77
Grosz, George 34, 85, 102, 124
Grunewald 113
Gutshow, Arvid 91
Guttman, Simon 129

Hagemeyer, Johan 104
Hahn, P. E. 85
Haldane, J. B.S. 116
Hammer und Sichel 109
Hardy, Bert 115
d'Harnoncourt, Réné 81
Harrisson, John 124, 130
Harrisson, Tom 120
Hartlaub, G. F. 103
Hauptmann, Gerhart 97
Hausmann, Raoul 102
Havinden, Ashley 121
Havinden, John 24, 121, 128, 129
Heartfield, John 34, **74,** 78, 85, 92, 102, 122
Hege, Walter 124
Heise, Carl Georg 5, 9, 81, 83, 95, 99, 105, 123, 125, 128
Hemingway, Ernest 79
Henri, Florence **37,** 124, 126, 130
Hepworth, Barbara 115
Hielscher, Kurt 97
Hildebrand, Hans 77, 78
Hill, D. O. 77, 117
Hitler Youth 47
Höch, Hannah 35, **76,** 85, 102
Hoernle, Edwin 6, 47
Hoppé, E. O. 101, 116, 117, 122
Howard, Brian 113, 115, 118, 124

Hoyningen-Huene, George de 35, 113, 116, 117, 127
Hubschmann (Hutton), Kurt 129
Huxley, Julian 116

International Advertising Agency 122
International Style 77, 80
Isherwood, Christopher 113, 115, 116

James, R. Haughton 128
Janin, Jules 39
Joachim, Hans A. 89
Jurgens, Grethe 128

Kandinsky, Wassily 21
Kamera-Almanach 103, 106
Kamera, Die 111
Karl-Robert-Langewiesche 110
Kasak, Ludwig 79
Kasebier, Gertrude 101
Kästner, Wilhelm 89, 93
Kauffmann, Mikhail 116
Keiling, Will 104
Ker-Seymer, Barbara 24, **113,** 114, 115, 116, 118, 120, 121, 124, 128, 130
Kertesz, André 93
Kimball, Abbott 92
Kino und Photo-Ausstellung 110
Klee, Paul 11
Klinkhardt and Biermann 43, 110
Kollmann, Franz 90
Kölnische Illustrierte 108
Köpfe des Alltags 6, 61, 65, 67, 117, 118
Kracauer, Siegfried 107
Kramer, Rudolf 123
Kraszna-Krausz, Andor 5, 35, 86, 126, 129, 130
Krull, Germaine 72, 93, 125
Kuehn, Heinrich 101
Kunstblatt, Das 77, 78, 83, 102, 107
Kunstchronik, Die 77

Land der Deutschen, Das 90
Lang, Fritz 116
Last Days of St. Petersburg 86
Lechenberg, Harald 119
Léger, Fernand 78
Leicester Galleries 24
Leipziger Anzeiger 39
Lerski, Helmar, 6, 7, 35, **60,** 61, 63, 64, 65, **66,** 67, 117, 118, 124, 128
Lewis, Wyndham 113
Lex, Alice 90, 101
Lichtbild, Das exhibition 94
Lichtwork 71
Life and Letters Today 115
Life 80
Light Play: Black, White, Gray 84
Lilliput 124
Linder, Paul 84
Linfert, Carl 94
Lissitzsky, El 37, 43, 78, 79, 84, 85
Listener, The 130
Little Review, The 84
London Promenade 124
Lorand, Robert 121
Lorant, Stefan 109, 124, 129
Lotar, Eli 102, 104
Lyddon, Hanford and Kimball 93

Macpherson, Kenneth 6, 65, 115, 117
Magazin, Das 108
Malerei der Neuen Sachlichkeit 103
Malerei Fotographie Film 43, 79, 80, 83, 89, 103
Malevich, Kasimir 80
Malik Verlag 34

Man, Felix H. 108, 116, 129
Man with a Movie Camera 86
Mann, Thomas 105
Mass Observation 120
MA ('Today') group 79
Mauritius-photo 92
Mayor Gallery 124
McGregor, Helen 120
McKnight-Kauffer 121, 130
Mellor, David 5, 6, 7, 113
Mendelsohn, Erich **88**, 89. 90. 129
Menschen ohne Maske 105
Metropolis 116
Mewes, George 127
Mills, G. H. Saxon 128
Modern Photography 128, 129, 130
Modern Publicity 130
Modotti, Tina **48. 50**
Moholy, Lucia 103, 110, 115, 121, 129
Moholy-Nagy, Laszlo 20, 35, 37, 40, 43, 72, 78, 79, 80, 83, 84, 85, 89, 90, 91, 101, 102, 103, 104, 106, 110, 115, 121, 123, 124, 127, 129
Molderings, Herbert 6, 7, 87
Molzahn, Johannes 107
Morris, Nancy 114
Morris, William 77
Mortimer, F. J. 115, 123, 128
Münchner Illustrierte Presse 108, 109, 115
Munkacsi, Martin **100**, 111, 108, 124
Münzenberg, Willi 6, 51, 92, 109
Museum of Modern Art, New York 83
Muthesius, Hermann 104

Nash, Paul 5, 23, 120, 124, 127, 130
Nerlinger, Oskar 90, 102
Nettelbeck, Walter 109
Neue Bild, Das 45
Neuer Deutscher Verlag 92
Neue Sachlichkeit, Die group 83
Neue Wege der Photographie 110
Neutra, Richard 80
New Gallery 116
Newhall, Beaumont 6, 7, 77
New York Art Center 93
Niépce, Nicéphore 96
Nierendorf, Karl 5, 17, 118, 124, 128
Non-Objective World, The 80
Nurnberg, Walter 118, 121, 123, 129

Object of the Photograph, The 40
Omnibus 128
Orbis Terrarum 97
Osram 120, 127
Oud, O. J. P. 77
Outerbridge, Paul 35, 83, 108.

Pabst, G. W. 117, 118
Painting Photography Film see *Malerie Fotographie Film*
Pantok, Bernhard 78
Panter, Peter 122
Park, Bertram 130
Parry, Roger 102
Passion of Joan of Arc, The 86
Penrose Annual 130
Peterhans, Walter 37, 110
Petschow, Robert 90
Pflanze als Lebewesen 91
Philpott, Glyn 113
Photo-Eye 5, 6, 7, 29, 37, 40, 77, 80, 85, 111, 115, 118, 120, 123, 125, 127, 130
Photograms of the Year 128, 129, 130
Photographie 126, 127, 128
Photographie ohne Kamera 84
Photographieren von Blüten, Das 103

Photographische Rundschau 81, 84
Photography 127, 129, 130
Photography Today 121, 123, 124, 130
Pick, Frank 123
Picture Post 116
Picturesque Germany 97
Posters and Publicity Yearbook 129, 130
Professional Photographers Association 130
Proletarian Photography 52
Publicity Club of London 128
Pudovkin, Vladimir 71, 86, 116

Querschnitt, Der 117, 124, 128

Randolph, B. W. 107
Ray, Man 35, 40, 77, 78, 84, 85, 86, 102
Reeck 110
Reichsarchiv Potsdam 35
Renger-Patzsch, Albert **2**, 5, 6, 7, **8**, 9, 10, 11, 12, 13, **14**, 15, 35, **73**, 79, 83, 89, 91, 92, **94**, 95, 96, 97, 98, 99, 101, 102, 103, 104, 105, 110, 111, 118, 120, 121, 123, **125**, 126, 127, 128, 129
Riefenstahl, Leni 100
Richter, Hans 78, 86, 111
Rodchenko, Alexander 91
Roh, Franz 5, 7, 29, 37, 38, 39, 43, 77, 81, 85, 106, 111, 115, 118, 125, 128, 130
Rossler, Jaroslav 102
Rothenstein, John 130
Royal Photographic Society, The 37, 127, 128
Ruttman, Walter 116

Salomon, Erich **108**, 122, 124, 129
Salon of 1857 73
Sander, August 6, 7, **54**, 55, 58, **70**, 71, 102, 105, 106
Schenk, Greta Overbeck 128
Schintling, Karl von 97, 98
Schonheit der Technik 90
Schopenhauer 39,. 70
Schrimpf, Georg 128
Schule Reimann 123
Schwarz, Heinrich 77
Schwarz, Rudolf 90
Schwitters, Kurt 78, 85
See Sand Sonne 91
Seiwert, Franz 106
Sembach, Klaus Jürgen 98
Sheeler, Charles 78, 83, 104
Shell-Mex 120, 123
Short History of Photography, A 69
Soby, James Thrall 86
Sommer, Karl 90
Sontag, Susan 96, 105
Spender, Humphrey 115, 116, 117, 118, **119**, 120, 122, 124, 129
Spender, Michael 115
Spender, Stephen 113, 115, 116, 118, 129
Spengler, Oswald 113
Spring 116
Springorum 40
Stankowski, Anton 126
Steichen, Edward 78, 81, 83
Stein, Gertrude 115
Steiner, Ralph 83, 108
Stenger, Erich 80
Stieglitz, Alfred 108
Stokoe, Brian 6, 7. 95
Stone, Sacha 35, 72, 127
Stotz, Gustav 35, 77, 79
Strand, Paul 108
Strasser, Alex 129
Studio, The 130
Style 1930 98
Styrsky, Jindrich 102

Tabard, Maurice 102
Talbot, W. H. Fox 80, 84, 96
Tanqueray, Paul 116, 129
Tchelitchew, Pavel 86
Technische Schönheit 90
Ten Days That Shook The World 86
Times, The 123, 127, 128, 130
transition 115
Tschichold, Jan 5, 37, 43, 77, 78, 81, 85, 118, 121, 130
Tudor-Hart, Edith 129
Turksib 66, 116
Tzara, Tristan 72, 84, 102

UFA 122
ufa-photo 92
Uhu 104
Ullstein Verlag 122
Umbehr, Otto (Umbo) 35, 110, 116
Unit 1 120
Urformen der Kunst 5, 17, 20, **22**, 23, 91, 105, 118, 123, 127

Van Den Bogaerde, U. 123
Van Der Rohe, Mies 77
Vanity Fair 83
Variété 69
Variety 86
Vernon, C. Harold 120, 130
Vertov, Dziga 86
Viertel, B 117
Vogue 81, 83
Volks-Illustrierte, Die 110

Wadman, Howard 130
Wadsworth, Edward 113, 120, 130
Walter, Hedda 35

Warstatt, Willi 106
Weber, Max 108
Weber, Wolfgang 108
Wegweisung der Technik 90
Wellington, Robert 23, 127
Wells, H. G. 116
Welt ist schön, Die 5, 8, 9, 72, 83, 90, 91, 95, 98, 99, 105, 110, 123, 126
Werkbund, Deutsche 6, 29, 35, 77, 78, 85, 86, 93, 104, 105, 111
Werkbund, Schweizer 78
Werk, Das 90
Wertheim Gallery 128
Weston, Brett 81, 85
Weston, Edward 35, 78, 80, 81, 83, 84
White, Clarence H. 108
White Hell of Piz Palu, The 100, 118
Wiene, Robert 86
Wiertz, Antoine 73, 75
Wieynck, H. 106
Wigman, Marie 113
Wildman, Shaw 129
Wilenzki 23
Wolff, Paul 91, 122, 128
Worker Photographers 6, 7, 92, 109
Workers International Relief 52, 109
World is Beautiful, The see *Welt ist schön, Die*
Worringer, Wilhelm 106
Wundergarten der Natur 91
Wurttembergische Polizeipräsidium 35

Zielke, Willy 92
Zuber, René 102
Zwart, Piet 78
Zwemmers 22, 23, 116, 118, 123, 124, 127